LANDFALL 236

November 2018

Editor Emma Neale
Founding Editor Charles Brasch (1909–1973)

Cover: Justin Spiers, *Dene*, 2017

Published with the assistance of Creative New Zealand

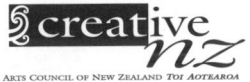

OTAGO UNIVERSITY PRESS

CONTENTS

4	Landfall Essay Competition 2018 Judge's Report,	*Emma Neale*
8	The Great Ending,	*Alice Miller*
15	Shining Through the Skull,	*Susan Wardell*
25	Chip Shop Girl,	*Antonia Bale*
32	Festival Highlight,	*Vincent O'Sullivan*
33	Epiphanies, Half Price,	*Vincent O'Sullivan*
34	Watching Ants,	*Sudha Rao*
35	An Afternoon in the Universal Café, Mumbai,	*Harry Ricketts*
36	Pink Blanket,	*Harry Ricketts*
37	Pagans,	*John Summers*
49	No Vacancy,	*Doc Drumheller*
50	Celebrants,	*Briar Wood*
52	Tohunga Suppression Act 1907,	*C.A.J. Williams*
53	Release,	*Jillian Sullivan*
55	Obiter Dicta,	*Philip Armstrong*
57	On Hume's Table,	*Megan Kitching*
58	I, Tambour,	*Rose Whitau*
60	A Thai-Chinese Stay-at-Home Mother Gets Political,	*Aiwa Pooamorn*
63	Dunedin Winter,	*Jilly O'Brien*
64	ART PORTFOLIO	*Justin Spiers*
73	Babes in the Woods,	*Heidi North*
79	Ode to Pomegranate,	*Joy Holley*
81	A Good Man,	*John Prins*
87	Tualima/Hand tattoo,	*Tusiata Avia*
89	South (from N.E.W.S. from the twenty-ninth floor),	*Ciaran Fox*
90	Facebook Sends a Memory,	*Victor Billot*
91	Experiments Touching Cold (1),	*Bryan Walpert*
93	Someone Other than Yourself,	*Siobhan Harvey*
94	The Sheepshed of Earthly Delights,	*Madeleine Child*
95	echidna: born of eve and lucifer,	*essa may ranapiri*
96	echidna: half woman half snake,	*essa may ranapiri*
97	1970 Something,	*Michael Hall*
98	Love Letter,	*Jodie Dalgleish*
99	The Bride from Clarry's Vineyard,	*Frankie McMillan*
100	A Matter of Timing,	*Elizabeth Kirkby-McLeod*

101	Aerodynamics, *Trevor Hayes*
102	The Jacket, *Thom Conroy*
108	The Mirror, *Helen Yong*
109	Thirteen Ways, *Kerry Hines*
112	Earth Day, *Therese Lloyd*
113	Time-travel TV Series, *Jane Arthur*
114	Study of Lizards, *Angela Trolove*
116	Sightsplain (1), *René Harrison*
117	Precise Edges, *Jess Mackenzie*
120	Flickering Between Shadow and Light, *Michael Mintrom*
122	Untitled, *Lissa Moore*
123	The Folding Map, *David Gregory*
124	The White Chairs, *Jessica Le Bas*
126	The Catch, *Iain Twiddy*
127	Naughty Boys' Island, *James Norcliffe*
128	ART PORTFOLIO *Susan Te Kahurangi King*
137	Hector, *Breton Dukes*
146	By the Roots, *Di Starrenburg*
159	What Happened, *Alan Roddick*
161	Delivery, *Lindsay Rabbitt*
162	Lines to Meaning, *Jasmine Taylor*
163	Dog with its Head out a Window, *Richard Reeve*
164	Caselberg Trust International Poetry Prize 2018 Judge's Report, *David Eggleton*
166	you can't be here, *Derek Schulz*
168	Full Measure, *Tony Beyer*

THE LANDFALL REVIEW

170 LANDFALL REVIEW ONLINE: Books recently reviewed / 172 MARK BROATCH on *This Mortal Boy* by Fiona Kidman / 175 TOM BROOKING on *Strangers Arrive* by Leonard Bell / 179 JANET CHARMAN on *Telling the Real Story* by Erin Mercer / 184 GAIL PITTAWAY on *Gabriel's Bay* by Catherine Roberston / 186 GINA COLE on *Freelove* by Sia Figiel / 189 MICHAEL HARLOW on *Athens to Aotearoa*, eds Diana Burton, Simon Perris and Jeff Tatum / 194 EMMA GATTEY, AWHINA CLARKE-TAHANA AND JACINTA RURU on *Juridical Encounters* by Shaunnagh Dorsett

202 Contributors
208 LANDFALL BACK PAGE John Z Robinson

EMMA NEALE

Landfall Essay Competition 2018 Judge's Report

In the *New Yorker* in May last year, Jia Tolentino argued that political and social pressures meant the online boom in personal essays was over.¹ Yet many New Zealand/Aotearoa writers—on the evidence of this contest—still seem to agree with Virginia Woolf's view that an essay, brilliant or profound, dealing with anything 'from the immortality of the soul to the rheumatism in your left shoulder … is primarily an expression of personal opinion'.²

Even if we accept that an essay's subject, no matter the costume, is the essayist—the genre is immensely protean. It might explore medical crisis, or expound on the diversity of sex lives in aquatic animals. It can collect factual evidence to support a political argument; it can run so seamlessly in poetry's slipstream that it seems camouflaged as poetry itself.

As Woolf says elsewhere, compared to the poem or the novel, the essay is an almost formless form. In the year she wrote this, 1905, the novel and the poem might have been easier to define—'A novel has a story, a poem rhyme'—but even if we expand our definitions of these, her question about the essay still holds:

> but what art can the essayist use in these short lengths of prose to sting us wide awake and fix us in a trance which is not sleep but rather an intensification of life?³

In other words, there is not much an essay *must* have. It doesn't need a narrative; it doesn't need prosody or line breaks; it doesn't even need an argument. It can be, in the words of one of New Zealand's most prominent new essayists, Ashleigh Young, an existential meditation; an exploration of shifting angles; something that can enact the way a mind shapes thought.⁴

Yet that last quality is something poetry excels at, too—so when it comes to spotting genres from the post-postmodern cycle lane, it can feel as if we're trapped on a roundabout, never able to make a smooth, non-perilous exit out of a circular argument.

There were 90 anonymous submissions to *Landfall*'s 2018 essay competition: an increase by around a third from 2017. By the time I had read about 60 essays that adhered to the idea that the self was the true subject, I began to want work that, if it did focus on memoir, could also use the experience as a gateway to travel elsewhere; as a way into understanding a culture, a social climate, a time, a wider phenomenon.

The catch even then, of course, is that style and craft have to be finely burnished: the 'argument' or opinion backed up with crisp and credible evidence; the comparisons having persuasive links; the conclusions clearly earned by what's come before. Some essays with considerable potential were let down by glitches in such things: by small eruptions to the trance, like, say, a closing image that jarred against or even dismantled the careful preceding argument or vision; or by the usual visual and semantic pollution of garbled grammar; an inflamed rash of typos; quotations not really illustrating a point; illogical comparisons; participles dangled as clownishly and boorishly as large fake foam penises waved out student car windows at the end of semester.

Even within the predominantly autobiographical narrative essays entered this year, there was a radiant and often deeply affecting spectrum of topics: from coping with Bell's Palsy to struggling with the conflict between the need to earn a wage and being implicated in environmental harm; from learning te reo as an adult Māori to the cultural and personal significance of wearing traditional sarees; from dealing with bullying at school to an apparently inherited obsession with chopping wood; from alcoholism to planning for the apocalypse. I sometimes felt like the invisible priestess at a busy confessional and was in equal parts shaken, uplifted and in awe of all I had been told.

First Place
Alice Miller's 'The Great Ending' impressed with its teeming yet elegantly controlled catalogue of international and national, Pākehā and Māori historical events; for the lyricism of the prose which glides from moments of understated comedy to those of stark horror—all the contraries held in a delicate web that says that we humans contain and withstand multitudes; that out of our shared and personal history we struggle and try to rise; that we are composed of such innocence and futility, such vision and foolishness, tragedy and desire. The essay uses the catalogue

and a lyrical style to evoke complexity and simultaneity—it achieves both lament and a kind of guarded eulogy. It lifts its focus to the retreating horizon of history, pulling it closer in the way it colours the telling with plangent grace.

Second Place
Susan Wardell's 'Shining Through the Skull' achieves something of a paradox: it was perhaps the most intimate of the personal narratives submitted, yet the one that also manages most successfully to hold the confessional in balance with its forays into other social territory: exploring what its central image—a woman's shaven skull—means in a selection of cultural, artistic and religious contexts. The writing glints with poetry as it also touches down on a number of potent themes, darting away again in a manner that emphasises the burning coals beneath: ambition, religion, vanity, charity, privacy, exploitation, the pitfalls in the anonymity of the internet, consent, shame, sexual fetishes. It seems more powerful than many of the other submitted 'abreactive memoirs'[5] in that the writer leaves us with a frisson of uncertainty at the end, knowing that the discomfiting central experience hasn't been fully defused by the telling of the tale, even though the telling shows such poise and fluency.

Third Place
Sam Keenan's 'Bad Girls' again is on the one hand a personal memoir; yet on the other an initially wry, quiet, searching—and increasingly chilling—documentary of a place, an era, a generation: specifically Westport in the 1980s; more generally New Zealand for young women in the same decade. The memory of a murdered babysitter sits in grim tension against the upbeat feminist rhetoric of the day—Girls Can Do Anything. In Keenan's hands, the slogan is shown up as wishful thinking, and we see how the very real and terrifying violence of misogyny shapes identities, destinies, edicts in the home, and how differing temperaments internalise a period's social tensions in any number of painful, destructive ways. Keenan's apparently lo-fi, low-key ending deftly etches an ongoing learned vigilance and unease; her entire piece cuts to the quick of value judgements like good girls bad girls, blame and choice.

Two essays were highly commended.

'Aquae Populus' by **Toby Buck** stood out for its crisp, vivid, colloquial pen portraits of members of a loosely connected community. It keeps a gently admiring and yet also cautiously sceptical eye on a shifting carousel of local identities. The writer is himself both entertained by and actively engaged with trying to read and understand human character, the nature of social groups in an unusual setting, and how outside economic forces contribute to the make-up of the clientele in the slightly odd context of the sauna: that intimate yet public space.

'That's Not a Māori Name: Penelope Fitzgerald's Aotearoan adventure', by **Derek Schulz**, reminds me of how a literary topic, in confident and generous hands—that is, hands that accept its readership might not all be immersed in the latest high-octane yet recondite theory—can pique curiosity and fascinate in its own right. I've read some of Fitzgerald's novels, but not the main short story explored here: yet that fact didn't affect my absorption in and enjoyment of this work, which lightly binds the essayist's memoir to his reading; recording, say, the emotional impact of reading about mania as a mania sufferer. The essay made me want to ferret out more of Fitzgerald's work, to test my own judgement and opinions against the essayist's. It also made me want to hunt for more such lyrical and illuminating literary criticism from Derek Schulz.

A further five essayists were commended: **Bryan Walpert** ('One Eye Open'), **Justine Whitfield** ('The Klimt Bubbles'), **Kirsteen Ure** ('Puriri Moth'), **Jocelyn Prasad** ('Uncut Cloth') and **Nadine Hura** ('A Thing of the Heart').

Alice Miller wins $3000 and a year's subscription to *Landfall*.

Notes

1. Jia Tolentino, 'The Personal-Essay Boom is Over', New Yorker, 18 May 2017: www.newyorker.com/culture/jia-tolentino/the-personal-essay-boom-is-over
2. Virginia Woolf, 'The Decay of Essay Writing' (1905), in *Selected Essays*, ed. David Bradshaw (Oxford: Oxford University Press, 2008).
3. Virgina Woolf, 'The Modern Essay' (1925), ibid.
4. See 'Ashleigh Young—5 Questions', on 'These Rough Notes—VUP News', 2 August 2016: http://victoriauniversitypress.blogspot.com/2016/08/ashleigh-young-5-questions.html
5. I've borrowed the term from Robert Atwan, series editor of *The Best American Essays*; specifically the David Brooks edited volume from 2012.

ALICE MILLER

The Great Ending

1918

1.
The story of the great ending begins with a mistake and ends with a miracle.

On 8 November a century ago, when the announcement came that the Great War was over, it was dusty in Balclutha. Dust from running children, dust from motor cars, dust from men's shoes as their owners ran down the main street, blowing tin whistles. All the townspeople were out of doors. 'It was as if,' a journalist wrote, 'a highly strung violin string had snapped':

> every bell clanged its utmost, whistles blew incessantly, and every empty petrol tin in the precincts of the town seemed to be called into service. A favourite practice was to tie a string of tins to a motor car or cycle and set off at a good bat up the street. A scratch band was raised, and, with tin whistles, trumpets and syrens, this was an effective, though unmusical, addition to the outburst of sound.

When the crowd were told that the report was premature—that in fact, the Great War had not yet ended, the armistice was still not signed—the mood didn't change. 'The general feeling was that if the armistice was not signed, it jolly well ought to be, seeing that we had gone so far.'

Four days later, there was still some uncertainty:

NO NEWS YET

GERMAN SURRENDER CONFIDENTLY PREDICTED
SHOULD GERMANS REFUSE TERMS
WILL BATTER THEM INTO SUBMISSION

—*Otago Daily Times*, 12 November 1918

Thursday's mistake had made everyone nervous. But by 9am the government confirmed that the armistice was signed at last. The national headlines became bolder: GERMANY OUT OF THE WAR; GREAT WAR ENDED; JOY ALL OVER THE WORLD.

Finally, the real celebrations could commence. In the small, landlocked town of Levin, there was an ambitious two-day programme planned. The signal would be given by the ringing of all bells, including the firebell and buglers in motor cars. All flags were to be hoisted, and all cars, bicycles and other vehicles to be carefully decollated for the parade. At 3pm the grand procession would assemble in Post Office Square.

The procession was ordered into 14 groups, beginning with returned soldiers in uniform, followed shortly after by TRAINING FARM BOYS AND PATRIOTIC AND RED CROSS WOMEN. The last two groups in the procession were NATIVES IN NATIVE COSTUME and CITIZENS IN DECORATED CARS.

But that Monday, the end of the war was not the only news. From London came the report that a game of soldiers' rugby football between Australia Headquarters and New Zealand Headquarters had been won by New Zealand.

A steamer travelling from San Francisco to Manila had been struck by lightning. Forty out of forty-six of the crew were missing.

Closer to home, Mrs M. Moody of 69 Roxburgh Street 'was walking along Lambton-quay, just outside the Gear Company's shop, when she slipped and fell, fracturing her left leg. John Condon, a fireman on the ferry steamer, fell in Abel Smith-street and suffered severe concussion by striking his head on the pavement.'

And in Vulcan Lane in Auckland, the well-known secretary of the Takapuna Jockey Club was knocked down by a four-seater motor car. The car stopped with one of its front wheels resting on the man's abdomen. A number of bystanders helped to lift the car, and the secretary was rapidly extricated from underneath. His clothing was severely torn and he was dazed; however, his cigar remained lit and he continued to smoke.

There was another problem, that Monday, that overshadowed all others.

At one of Auckland's largest private hotels most of the staff were struck down by influenza, to the extent that several very distinguished guests took over the duties of the domestic servants. Some guests had to make their own beds. There was even the very odd spectacle of a titled gentleman working the lift.

Māori settlements in the north were badly hit by the epidemic. In many regions, hospitals were overflowing and schools were rapidly converted into hospitals. Many appointments were postponed, including the Church of

England annual sale, a card evening at the Bell Tea rooms, and the fancy-dress ball of the Arowhenua Maori Soldier Day Committee.

Lemons became wildly expensive. People of means were requested to donate citrus fruit. Those with motor cars were asked to lend them to the effort.

Schools were closed, as were moving picture theatres and ordinary theatres, dancing halls, billiard saloons, concert rooms and shooting galleries.

Children's demonstrations on Armistice Day were also postponed.

What stayed open late were chemists' shops. The shops quickly ran out of bottles, and urged the public to bring their own. They also requested that nobody follow the example of one particular (unnamed) lady, who ran into the chemist at the height of the epidemic, demanding cosmetic face powder.

Strangely, it was people in their twenties and thirties who were most susceptible to the influenza virus. Soldiers returned from months of foreign battle only to die from the flu. After death, bodies often turned dark purple or black.

Levin's Peace Programme, however, remained unaffected; influenza or not, the show would go on. Day Two of the Peace Programme consisted of a sports gathering and district picnic, all held at the Levin Park Domain, with numerous attractions including a Punch and Judy Show. Hot water, tea, milk and sugar were provided free of charge on the grounds. Guests brought their lunch, along with the family teapot.

The Fisk Jubilee Singers were still scheduled to sing at the Oddfellows' Hall on 13 November, with a programme featuring 'popular airs' and 'coon songs'.

The *Otago Daily Times* offered a useful suggestion for 'when you get into a frame of mind that makes life seem one tiresome duty after another'. The suggested product promised to 'tone up the entire system, help make the blood rich and red, strengthen the nerves, increase the appetite, put colour in the cheeks and lips, and drive away that unnatural feeling'. Just ask for Dr Williams' Pink Pills for Pale People.

A writer to the *Auckland Star* suggested that when a son reaches a 'critical age', a father should 'place in his hands a standard book of advice to young men, and let the mother act likewise for the daughter'. This being done, children will receive 'necessary knowledge re. their sexual nature ... in a safe and thorough manner'.

On the evening of Day Two of Levin's Peace Programme all shops were lit up. There was a monster torchlight procession from the post office at 7pm, a free impromptu concert, and the burning of an effigy of the Kaiser.

Towns everywhere had rigged up their own effigies, some adorned with an iron cross and 'ignonimously dangled'. The Kaiser was doused in petrol and set alight, and the townspeople cheered as he burned.

Lloyd George was quoted in the newspapers:

> In the spring we were being sorely pressed. The Channel ports were being threatened. The enemy steel was pointed at our hearts. It is now autumn. Constantinople is almost within gunfire. Austria is shattered and broken. The Kaiser and Crown Prince have abdicated, and a successor has not been found, but a regency proclaimed. This is the greatest judgment in history. Germany has a choice to-day, but she will have none to-morrow. She is ruined inside and outside ...

> Our terms must prevent a recurrence ... Let us banish faction. It would be unwise to forget. We must impose justice, Divine justice, which is the foundation of civilisation ... We are not going to repeat the folly of 1870.

In a letter to the editor, H.S. protested that while it is a fineable offence to discharge firearms, it will be found in the suburbs that there are more and more small boys with pea-rifles. The boys and their rifles are a regular commotion. It is well time these children's irresponsible parents were fined. The government must put a true end to the 'pea-rifle nuisance'.

Ladies' high-grade soft white hose were for sale: seamless; the best; all sizes; at the sale price of three shillings and one penny (postage two shillings extra).

The *Taranaki Daily News* announced that flouncings are in style once again. Morey's have a fine range of flouncing embroideries for ladies.

2.

Meanwhile, in Europe, *The Decline of the West* (*Der Untergang des Abendlandes*) was published. In it, Oswald Spengler argued that the Western world is at its end, and we are witnessing its final season—winter—before a new historical cycle. According to Herr Spengler:

The era of individualism, liberalism and democracy, of humanitarianism and freedom, is nearing its end. The masses will accept with resignation the victory of the Caesars, the strong men, and will obey them.

The Irish poet W.B. Yeats also believed that the world was operating on a cycle. In 1918 he and his wife were channelling spirits. Their proposed cycle was just over a thousand years long and divided into twelve sections. According to the Yeats' notes, in 1875 a period of 'war and abstractions' began. This lasted until 1927, with the 'elimination of intellect, Europe in artificial unity' (although this phrase ends with a question mark). Around 2050 there will be: 'adoration of force, decadence'.

The Yeats' research on these cycles would appear in one of his poems the following year. In early drafts of the poem, Yeats addressed the war directly—'the Germans are … now to Russia come'. He cut this line in his revision. The final version ends: 'And what rough beast, its hour come round at last,/ Slouches towards Bethlehem to be born?'

In Shrewsbury, England, on Armistice Day, the mother of Wilfred Edward Salter Owen—the young man who wrote 'In all my dreams, before my helpless sight,/ He plunges at me, guttering, choking, drowning'—received a telegram. The telegram said that regrettably, Wilfred had been killed fighting in France. He was 25 years old. When she received the telegram he had already been dead a week.

In neutral Switzerland the young Jorges Luis Borges had graduated from the Collège de Genève. 'You have wakened,' he would write, 'not out of sleep, but into a prior dream.'

3.
How would New Zealanders remember the war? The *Evening Post* suggested it would be recalled as the point when all women started smoking. Smokers included women frequenting great hotels and restaurants, but also those doing 'men's work'. 'Observe,' the journalist wrote, 'the habitual readiness and insouciance with which they whisk the case from pocket, close it with a snap, and lightly tap the cigarette on the back of the left hand before lighting up.'

Should we mention that when the armistice was announced in Albany, it was the thirty-first week of the second egg-laying competition? Or that the Williamstown Cup was won by Seabound, beating Red Signal by a neck?

There is one last story to remember, which was not reported in the papers. It happened on the day of the first, false armistice, 8 November.

On that afternoon a man witnessed a strange cloud, like a whirlwind, come towards him. He ran back towards his farmhouse, and felt something press heavily on his shoulders. He claimed he could see, stretching towards him, every one of the world's roads.

When he entered his family's house he couldn't speak. But something spoke through him: 'May peace be upon you,' the voice said. 'I am the Holy Spirit who is speaking to you; wash yourselves clean, make yourselves ready.'

The man cleared out his house and instructed others to do the same. He claimed to speak through the Holy Spirit or the archangel Gabriel or Michael. His family were not the only ones to believe he had gone mad. He took them walking over rough farmland at night, stumbling over piles of dirt. He separated out selected family members' belongings, and said they belonged to the dead.

Those whose belongings he separated out caught influenza and died. The ones he urged to leave their houses stayed alive. People began to listen.

While across the country a false armistice was celebrated, on the man's farm the healing began. First a dying man, after prayer, saw a needle emerge from his thigh and was cured. A girl who was bedridden walked again. By the end of 1918 Ratana's farm would have had many, many visitors—and 8 November was remembered as a day of revelation.

Shortly before his death, Jorges Luis Borges said to a hall of people: 'We do not read to discover the end. After all, people reread stories, so it is impossible to believe they read to discover how they will end.'

And in this great ending, we have our interruptions, starts; a mistake and a miracle. Premature announcements and divine revelations, a terrible illness and the promise of healing, straw men we string up and burn. Days of unfortunate falls, of women pressing cigarettes to insouciant lips, of flouncing and miracle pills and the stacking of blue bodies. Days when we shoot our pea-rifles into our neighbour's garden, and with strange clouds ahead, sing as loudly as we can, of dust that builds on dust.

References

Part 1

All the townspeople …; The general feeling was … 'Triumph's Tocsin', *Clutha Leader*, 12 November 1918

Four days later … 'No news yet', *Otago Daily Times*, 12 November 1918

The national headlines … 'Germany out of the war', *Evening Post*, 12 November 1918; 'The Great War ended', *Horowhenua Chronicle*, 12 November 1918

Finally, the real celebrations … 'Levin's peace programme', *Horowhenua Chronicle*, 12 November 1918

From London came the report … 'Football', *Wanganui Chronicle*, 12 November 1918

A steamer travelling … 'Struck by lightning', *Marlborough Express*, 12 November 1918

Closer to home … 'Two accidents', *Evening Post*, 12 November 1918

And in Vulcan Lane …; At one of Auckland's … 'Local and general', *Evening Post*, 12 November 1918

Māori settlements … 'Many residents attacked', *New Zealand Herald*, 12 November 1918

Many appointments were postponed … 'Town & country', *Timaru Herald*, 12 November 1918

Lemons became wildly … 'Clothing, fruit, cars', *Auckland Star*, 12 November 1918; 'The influenza epidemic', *Auckland Star*, 12 November 1918

Schools were closed … 'Places of amusement closed', *Evening Post*, 12 November 1918

Children's demonstrations … 'No children's gatherings', *Evening Post*, 12 November 1918

What stayed open late … 'Bring your own bottle', *Evening Post*, 12 November 1918

Strangely, it was people … James Belich, *Paradise Reforged* (London: Penguin, 2002); Molly Billings, 'The Influenza Epidemic', June 1997: http://virus.stanford.edu/uda/

Levin's peace programme … 'Levin's peace programme', *Horowhenua Chronicle*, 12 November 1918

The Fisk Jubilee Singers … 'Local and general', *Akaroa Mail and Banks Peninsula Advertiser*, 12 November 1918

The *Otago Daily Times* offered … 'Pale Pills', *Otago Daily Times*, 12 November 1918

A writer to the *Auckland Star* … 'Children's morals', *Auckland Star*, 12 November 1918

On the evening of Day Two … 'Levin's peace programme', *Horowhenua Chronicle*, 12 November 1918

Towns everywhere had rigged up … 'Prohibition in practice', *Taranaki Daily News*, 12 November 1918; 'Triumph's Tocsin', *Clutha Leader*, 12 November 1918

Lloyd George was quoted … 'Germany ruined', *Auckland Star*, 12 November 1918

In a letter to the editor … 'The pea-rifle nuisance', *Auckland Star*, 12 November 1918

Ladies' high-grade soft white hose … 'Untitled', *Otago Daily Times*, 12 November 1918

The *Taranaki Daily News* announced … 'Local and general', *Taranaki Daily News*, 12 November 1918

Part 2

Meanwhile in Europe … Oswald Spengler, *The Decline of the West*, 2 vols, trans. Charles Francis Atkinson, (New York: Alfred A. Knopf, 1922)

The Irish poet … William Butler Yeats, *The Collected Works of W.B. Yeats Volume XIII: A vision* (New York: Simon & Schuster, 2013)

The Yeats' research … Terence Brown, *The Literature of Ireland: Culture and criticism* (Cambridge: Cambridge University Press, 2010), 85

In Shrewsbury, England … 'Wilfred Owen's Shrewsbury home granted Grade II listing', *Guardian*, 29 December 2014

In neutral Switzerland … Jorges Luis Borges, *The Aleph*, trans. Andrew Hurley (New York: Penguin, 2004)

Part 3

The *Evening Post* suggested … 'Women smokers', *Evening Post*, 12 November 1918

Should we mention that … 'Egg-laying competition', *New Zealand Herald*, 12 November 1918

Or that the Williamstown Cup … 'Williamstown Cup', *Evening Post*, 12 November 1918

On that afternoon … Angela Ballara, 'Ratana, Tahupotiki Wiremu', from the Dictionary of New Zealand Biography: www.TeAra.govt.nz/en/biographies/3r4/ratana-tahupotiki-wiremu

First a dying man … Morrison, Paterson, Knowles, Rae, *Mana Māori and Christianity* (Wellington: Huia, 2012)

Shortly before his death … George Watson, 'An Unquenchable Gaiety of Mind', *American Scholar*, 31 May 2012

SUSAN WARDELL

Shining Through the Skull

The fontanelle is the most terrifying part of a newborn baby. My daughter was born with no hair—the merest hint of red-gold fuzz. I ran my fingers over her head, over the basin in the middle of her skull where bones did not yet meet. The site of her sentience. The skin there was hot with its own central pulse. A person I did not know yet, thrumming under my fingers. I could not breathe.

I was also born bald, and I have chosen to be made bald twice more: once for a cheering and charitable crowd, and once for an invisible audience I was too naïve to see.

I'll tell you about the first time I shaved my head. I was sixteen and the leader of my school's Christian group—an introverted, bass-playing over-achiever with plans to save the world. The long, dark hair flowed all the way down my back. I'd been growing it since kindergarten. I arranged the fundraiser with the local branch of CanTeen; made up some flimsy collection boxes by cutting slots into butter containers. A few shops around town agreed to put them on the counter. I took one to my school's office, my picture, loose-haired and half-smiling, taped to it. The principal's eyebrows hit the ceiling. 'Oh no, Susan, you shouldn't mutilate yourself like that!' I still remember the flush of shame, pulling my sleeves down over the year-old scars on my arms. 'There are other ways to fundraise, surely?'

'It's a slap in the face to people who really have cancer,' a favourite teacher cornered me in the hallway to say. I cried in the bathroom where I used to go with the yellow craft knife I had stolen from a friend. A third teacher had to allay my obvious distress by checking with a student a year below me who did have cancer. I received a blessing by proxy. But by then I knew the school didn't want a head girl with a 'mutilated' head, and that was a mantle I had hoped for.

I've always been an all-or-nothing kind of person. But extremes are not just about the more, they're also about the less. How low can I go? How much can I lose? When I was fourteen I wanted to be a martyr. I cherished a little book about the young people who had died at Columbine, Christ's name on their lips. I used to have dreams about being stood on a brick wall with a gun to my head. So in my dramatic teen mind, the time had come. I took a deep breath and followed through. Besides, the cool girls had started talking to me, whispering disbelief and solidarity in the hallways. I collected a paltry hundred dollars in gold coins. But if I am honest, the money had never been the point.

    On the big day I wore my favourite pink top and a string of cheap pearls. I sat between two strangers on a temporary stage in front of the railway station. There was a small crowd. My hair did not fall on the makeshift flooring that morning—it was divided and carefully tied, sliced off one little pigtail at a time. The neat locks were bagged up for a wig-maker. The final buzz was exhilarating. I felt reborn. I walked away grinning. Did you know that air has a texture? As I moved through the mild morning, I felt as if I were swimming through it. Like it had ripples, a grain. The next morning I stood up the front of my small church hall to lead the music, and I did not bow my head in prayer. Instead I tilted my face to the sky and felt God pour light down into my naked skull. Later my pastor told me it had been moving to see me up there like that. And so I moved out of my own body and into his eyes, and liked the view.

    On the street it was different. I felt guilty walking around town. What if strangers thought I had cancer? What right did I have to withdraw from that bank of public sympathies? I flew to a family wedding in Auckland with my dad. He phoned ahead to make sure no one thought I was dying, and I figured that at least then they wouldn't be talking about my parents' separation. But at the last moment I lost my nerve, searching my drawers for the thick dark wig my mum had once used to dress as Cleopatra. I itched and sweated all day. At the end of the night I took it off and felt amazing, sitting in the sparkling candlelight, free and bare. I danced with my father. I learned that being hairless could make me feel fearless.

My hair grew back. Hair does that. But that was only the first shave.

    It was six years later, and I had wasted no time. I had studied and graduated with first-class honours. I had travelled with my best friend to volunteer at the edge of a war zone—seeking better stories, and very nearly getting them. We missed out on a massacre in South Sudan by a mere 40km. I've milked that story a lot over the years. I don't tend to mention that we spent a good portion of the trip reading Christian romance novels and arguing over our one jar of peanut butter.

Back home I slipped compunctiously back into a middle-class student life. Then one day I got an email from my friend Regina. Regina who had real stories, who had fled Sudan as a child and grown up in a refugee camp. One of the sweetest, most self-effacing, hard-working people I've ever met, who now wanted to pursue development studies so she could go back home and help people. I had no money to respond. But I didn't fret long before I had the brilliant thought. My flatmate had recently made a big pile of cash shaving her head. There had been an advertisement on Student Job Search. I emailed someone called Justin who was 'overseas at present' but was willing to arrange it through his local contacts. They would pay me $800 to first film an 'unconventional' cut and then to do a full buzz. They would also have a photographer take pictures of the results for a 'beauty positive' alopecia awareness campaign. $800 goes a long way in South Sudan. I quickly set a date.

On the day I climbed an old staircase squeezed in between two storefronts. The photography studio above had a four-poster bed in one corner for boudoir shoots. The hairdresser was chatty and professional. I was wearing a black cocktail dress and heels, as instructed, and reminding myself that I'd done this before. Well, not exactly this. The hair fell to polished wood, and there was no applause.

I am not a hero, but I like to feel like a martyr. As my hair fell there, I imagined it falling at the feet of the worthiest woman in Africa. I suppose I hoped it would fit me for battle, bear me back into the 'good fight' alongside her. I have had a tendency to borrow the afflictions of others. I have a tendency to wear them as my own.

After the clippers came a new offer—an extra $100 if I got my head shaved back to smooth with cream and a razor. The procedure was specific: I had to request it on camera. I left with my skull cold and 'smoother than a newborn rat'.[1]

I proudly sent the money, with no specifics on its origin.

Regina was the one who taught me to cook beans. We had just two large pots, tended carefully over a tiny open fire, in an IDP camp in the middle of the savannah land. She didn't laugh or tsk when I burned the *mondazzi*. She called me 'sister' and patiently braided my wayward *mundu* hair. My head burned for two days with the tight twists she made so close to my scalp, and at night I lay awake beside her, determined not to say anything. I wanted so much to be her sister. It was only a couple of months after the second shave that I went back to East Africa, this time to do research for my doctorate. Great timing, I thought. Extremely practical for the heat. But I was working in the city this time, where I was dismayed to find the educated young Pentecostals I hoped to make friends with all had glossy, salon-treated hair. I stood up the front with an inch of un-styled fuzz and looked positively, paradoxically, poor. 'God will lead you to your place of prosperity,' the pastors preached while giving a side-eye to my obvious lack of ... faith? Femininity? Virtue?

> ... but that if a woman has long hair, it is her glory? For long hair is given to her as a covering.
> —1 Corinthians 11:15 (NLT)

Back home in the Anthropology Department, one of the other postgrads was also writing about Pentecostal women and what she called 'biblical feminism'.[2] She herself had left a fundamentalist background in the USA, started wearing trousers, cut her hair short, and then gone back to study them.

> For if a woman does not cover her head, she might as well have her hair cut off; but if it is a disgrace for a woman to have her hair cut off or her head shaved, then she should cover her head.
> —1 Corinthians 11:6 (NIV)

She told me about the women from United Pentecostal Church International who grow their hair sometimes to ankle length, even suffering back problems from its weight. Their uncut hair not only represents their faith but gives them authority to 'charge angels'—to make requests at the throne of God, to drape it over the sick and claim healing. As I listened I imagined those women, honey-lit in mid-western churches, praying (silently) as glory streams down their dark blonde mantles. Like fire, like melted amber. In my mind they became stained glass windows: *in memoriam*.

My husband tells a story about falling in love with the back of my head. I sat in front of him in a church pew at a youth group study night. We were fifteen and my hair was long and dark. When I planned to shave my head for a second time I was twenty-two and we were married. I asked him what he thought. He shrugged: 'It's your body.' In bed, after the deed was done, he gently ran his hand over the militant black fuzz that remained. We were both testing this out: the change, the thing gone, the thing revealed. 'That feels strange,' I told him. The tiny barbs velcroed to the pillow when I slept, sexless. It was a while before we learned the truth.

It happened on a car trip. I was chatting with a friend who had shaved her head not long after me. With the same people, in fact, and at my referral. It came up in conversation ... or came out, I should say. The ongoing emails. The online chats at odd hours. The uncomfortable questions. I'd been trying to politely ignore them for a couple of years by then. Starting with the email from 'Nicole', who was a stylist in town, wanting to ask if I would shave again. Offering me $1000. I declined. Then the magazine editors who wanted to shoot me for a cutting-edge cover: $1500 was mentioned. Then came salon owners planning a big live opening: $10,000. I exchanged a few emails. 'Just in case it's real,' I told my husband. No charitable impulse this time, when we had just $14 across all our accounts. The money had been real last time. But time wore on and nothing came of it until one day Justin offered to pay me again, for another head shave, another photo shoot. By then I'd had enough and politely (always politely) refused. He asked why I chose to get the first shave done. Whether I'd opted for the razor shave. When I said I couldn't remember, he sent me a screenshot from the video, where the hairdresser is poised above my bowed and newly bald head with a razor. My stomach felt strange.

'Is this you?' he asked.

'I have to go. I have an early start tomorrow.'

'Did you like the feeling of the blade on your head?'

You know those hairless cats that people enter into shows? Sphynx, the breed is called, with sloped eyes and folds upon folds of flesh in a pale, foetal pink. Axolotl pink. The pink of something dragged out of the dark, in the maw of something worse still.

It's not that there were *no* warning bells, you see, it's just that it's easy to get used to small fires. My friend's exchanges with these people were even more obviously 'off', I comforted myself by thinking. 'Do you usually shave your armpits?' they asked her. 'What do you use to shave your body hair?' She shut down the conversations much more quickly than I did.

Is this what happens when women talk to each other? When we pause our incessant, brave, blind 'just getting on with it'? 'What, you too?' we ask in surprise.

'Yes. Me too.'

Of course we began to wonder how many more women were out there. Where the images were really being sent. I considered making a file of all the messages and all the details we knew. Taking it to the police. But was there a crime? We had consented. (How much does one have to know to consent?) We had been paid. (Where is the line between exploitation and commerce?) Our hair was by then in cute shoulder-length bobs.

Besides, I was preoccupied with watching myself expand, encompass. Hearing my daughter's heartbeat, like the rush of little waves, inside the ocean of me. I left it at an uncomfortable curiosity. I got on with my life.

In the end the story found me before I found it. I opened my laptop one day and read the headlines: 'Dunedin student feels violated after finding picture on fetish website' and 'Bald backpacker funder plays down fetish connection'. I couldn't believe it. And yet, I completely could. The full scope of the operation never emerged; nor did the person behind an email chain from 'Gemma' to 'Muhammed' to 'Justin'. The story was much the same as mine among the few women the reporters talked to.

I broke the rule and read the comments. One anonymous pundit confirmed that it was 'pretty obvious' and 'the way the ad reads is definitely sketchy'. You'd have to be 'dumb as a stump' not to tweak to it being for a fetish website, someone else says. My chest tightens, reading this. Writing it now. I remind myself that I finished my PhD at age twenty-five. That I've won awards. Been published. I remind myself of this and yet my chest stays tight. 'It's not like they even had to get their tits out, so I can't see why there would be any shame really,' another random commentator confirms. Yes. Yes. My mind swims around and around that pool of revelation, looking for the tap left on. The source of the shame. I can't seem to find it. I just know I'm swimming in it.

Did I mention that I liked the photos they took of me? I put them on Facebook. I thought I looked fierce and beautiful—lips pinked, lashes long, head unapologetically bare and tilted curiously at the camera. They had posed me well. I have always enjoyed posing. They were classy photos. But dark roots soon reclaimed the bare skin.

Am I wounded? I don't think so. Embarrassed? Yes, that. The line between innocence and naivety is purple and taut. It is vanity that shames me. That I'd thought I was the cover-girl and ended up the pin-up girl, or something less than that. That people I don't know are panting as they watch my head being slowly bared. They are probably paying for it. I wonder how much.

'What do you notice first about a person when you meet them?' I remember a friend asking a group of us, perched around a bench outside our imposing brick high school. We were thirteen, priming ourselves for this new kind of noticing and being noticed. 'Eyes,' someone says. Others agree. 'Confidence,' someone else adds. 'Hair' is the honest, simple answer I would not speak. The first thing I would notice. Blonde, brunette, redhead. (Did my inner monologue read like a bad joke?) Short, long. Curly, straight. Bald.

What is it about baldness that is so titillating? I wonder now. Can the fetishists even explain it themselves? As if desire comes with a roadmap through the synapses. Over the skin. In primary school I resolved that I wanted to be beautiful, not hot. I had a feel of 'beautiful' that I couldn't yet communicate. It was something to do with swans and flowers. Gowns and long hair. It was clean and pale as the moon.

Now the pale moon of my head brought a rise to a stranger through the screen. What's that to me? What does it matter? Would I still have considered it if I knew the purpose of those photos? If I was paid more? Do I regret it? I don't know. Or perhaps I just can't answer, even to myself. In her poem 'Hairless', Jo Shapcott questions whether the bald can lie. 'The nature of the skin says not,' she answers:

> it's newborn-pale, erection-tender stuff,
> every thought visible—pure knowledge,
> mind in action—shining through the skull.

I imagine myself seated at a large dinner table with a group of bald women. Joan of Arc sits to my left, a wine glass cocked in her long hands. Jo March is on my right, sampling cheese. Fantine sits across from us, applying black lipstick, as Furiosa makes everyone laugh with biting comments about politicians. Grace Jones beside her, already quite drunk, is snorting as she makes a small monument with the salt shakers. Evey smiles, her mouth wide. We drink and laugh. We plan a revolution of proud, shaved women walking tall through bloody streets. The wine spills.

What is it about bare skin that always recalls violence? Is it the implication of a blade? Or simply the paring down of the ornamental, like the ritualised removal of garments, of jewellery, before a fight: 'Jesus, hold my earrings!'³ The shedding of personal identifiers that make it easier to harm, easier to be harmed.

On my first visit to the Human Anatomy museum it is the eyelashes that get me. The eyelashes and other places where the skin is left on. The knuckles where thick gold hair loops in tiny tensile arches against cavernous pores. A face, in citrine sections, where one corner slice bears a five o'clock shadow. Frozen at 5pm now for five years. Fifteen years. More. I wonder whose job it is to shave the dead.

The job of poetry is to make beautiful what we cannot bear to know. To tell the truth, shorn and holy. But as the poet said, humankind cannot bear very much reality. The job of a woman's hair is to style and fuss over the top of what we cannot bear to see: her raw, corporeal self, so often stripped against her will. At the end of the Second World War, French women accused of collaborating with or sleeping with German soldiers were stripped and beaten and their heads shaved. No trial, just mob justice. They were called *les femmes tondues*—the shorn women.

I do not know what it is liked to be stripped against my will. By illness. By enemies. By friends. Yet for a time, I too was a shorn woman: defined by what I lacked.

There is a horrible vulnerability in a bare head, with its so-thin dermis and the dark pound of blood so near the surface. Head wounds always bleed a lot. They won't keep quiet.

So, what of the choice to bare oneself on purpose? To fiercely pre-empt the violence of the world? I think of the protests where women walk naked down the street. Each bare step claims 'I am safe here.' I see their photos in my stream and still some part of me just wants to wrap them in blankets. They look cold and soft, even with brave chins tilted, hands busy with signs that say (without words): 'You can't touch me.' But I'm afraid, so afraid, that's not true.

> She is clothed with strength and dignity, and she laughs without fear of the future
> —Proverbs 21:35

Britney Spears' shave is said to be a marker of her sad decline into mental disarray. Grace Jones' bald head is heralded as a radical rejection of mainstream femininity. It's only when we shave our own heads that we are dangerous—pitiable or powerful. Shaved against our will, we are easier to make into saints or whores. Or both. Indeed, Fantine's final 'choice' to take to the streets is marked by this, and as a voyeur to that particular misery it is hard to disentangle the shock of the indignity from the horror of her submission to it. Anne Hathaway, who plays Fantine in the 2012 movie, described sobbing 'inconsolably' in one of the most intense moments of her career as her hair was hacked off on camera. She too was paid for this, and a million strangers have watched her do it, the moment immortalised in perfect digital fidelity. When Emma Gonzales, Parkland shooting survivor, stepped in front of the world's cameras, she was both strong and tearful in a khaki jacket and a buzz cut. She became an internet icon almost immediately. Later she revealed that she'd cut her hair purely for practical reasons in the hot Florida summer. She'd had to make a PowerPoint presentation to convince her parents to let her do it.

'Language cannot do everything,' Adrienne Rich writes, and yet we are caught between this and 'a silence that strips bare'.[4] Rich describes a moment in Carl Theodor Dreyer's 1928 silent film *The Passion of Joan of Arc* (starring Renée Jeanne Falconetti) where:

> Falconetti's face, hair shorn, a great geography
> mutely surveyed by the camera
>
> If there were a poetry where this could happen
> not as blank spaces or as words
>
> stretched like skin over meanings
> but as silence falls at the end.

Is baldness a silence, then, or a statement? Does it say something for us or about us? I have shaved my head for money. I have shaved my head for charity. I have shaved my head for someone else's sexual pleasure, though I did not know it at the time. My daughter is four years old now, fontanelle long since closed, and she wears her hair thick and long like her mama's. Like dark gold. I wonder, will I tell her this story? For as I think of it again, I find that I have to work to stretch the meaning of my dignity, like skin, over the electric tangle of circumstance, choice, intention and result beneath. Can you see it all shining there? My hair is long. My skull still feels bare.

Notes

1   Desireé Dallagiacomo (2015), 'Shave Me' from Button Poetry: www.youtube.com/watch?v=9uYTENfTO1s
2   Sherrema Bower (2015), '"A Woman's Glory": A study exploring experiences of spiritual power and the gendered lives of women in two Pentecostal communities in the USA and New Zealand', PhD thesis: https://ourarchive.otago.ac.nz/bitstream/handle/10523/6765/BowerSherrema2015PhD.pdf?sequence=1&isAllowed=y
3   Gem Wilder (2017), 'Jesus', Turbine: http://turbinekapohau.org.nz/2017-contents-poetry-gem-wilder/
4   Adrienne Rich (1975), 'Cartographies of Silence': https://poetrying.wordpress.com/2008/12/15/cartographies-of-silence-adrienne-rich/

ANTONIA BALE

Chip Shop Girl

It was on the news again, their town. The camera zeroed in on the main drag. Swung past the war memorial and the Four Square, came to a stop outside A1 Chip n Curry. Everyone at school called it the A1 Double C. Like a bra size or something.

'Badly beaten, the man remains in intensive care,' the TV man said.

They showed the chip shop door with its brightly coloured bead curtain. The sign on the door said closed but Shona could almost hear it: the way each little bead twinkled when you ran your fingers across it, the ones on the bottom gently scraping the tiles on the floor.

It wasn't enough to see it, she thought. You had to smell that place to really know it. The fat from the fryers, the chapatis, the burgers. It'd stay in your hair for days if you let it.

They were showing faces of the ones that probably did it. A group of boys milling in the park. Some of them looked angry, but maybe they were just tired, bored, scared. If you looked too hard you could make those faces say anything, really.

The TV man was making out like it was a bad town. But Shona knew that wasn't it. She'd seen the sign sellotaped on the chip shop window, the word JOB written clearly. Tanya's job up for grabs, Shona's old one. Put two and two together. It wasn't a bad town if people were looking out for one another.

Behind her, sitting at the table in the dark, Mum fumbled with a lighter. There was a click and a hiss and then Shona could hear her inhaling.

Now they were showing a shot of her school gates, the concrete quad, the brick wall where the seniors smoked. The name of the school fuzzed out on the sign.

'That's your school, Ma!' said Dobbie to Shona, lolling on the sofa. His thumb was wedged in his mouth and his little legs were kicking against the head of a fluffy giraffe.

'Don't suck your thumb,' Shona said to her son.

'Switch it off,' said Mum.

'Pipe down,' growled Uncle.

Shona bit her nails. The TV man was talking about something else now. A storm somewhere, people piled up on a boat in a rough sea. Bad things happening in other places.

'Time for bed,' said Mum, scooping up Dobbie. She pressed a hand on Shona's shoulder as she walked past. 'You too, love, you look tired.'

'She's all right,' said Uncle.

Shona thought of the tinkling beads.

Upstairs in her bedroom, the neck of the glass bottle felt warm in her hand, just right. The bottle clunked as she pulled it out from under her bed. She took a swig and her tongue recoiled like it always did at first. After a few lugs right there on her knees, she got up and climbed into bed, bringing the bottle in with her. She wedged it between her thighs and bent her face over it so she could breathe in the sharp smell.

'Slag,' Shona said. 'Stupid, stupid slag.'

She lurched the bottle toward her and took a big gulp, her tongue growing numb and fuzzy.

Uncle and Mum were yelling in the next room. Dobbie was crying. Then Mum's voice: *Look what you've done now.* A door slam.

The TV man had said it was appalling.

'Appalling,' Shona said, to see how it felt in her mouth. Ah—like a sound you might make without meaning to, and then lips pressing hard together, heavy tongue, hitting the top of your teeth first. Ah—Paul, a man's name—ling ling ling. Tongue flicking down, mouth open again, everything left hanging.

Quickest route from school was past the A1 Double C.

Shona finished off the rest of the bottle, slid under the covers and hugged it to her side like a hottie. She was on track now. Passing subjects, fitting the uniform again. She'd dyed her hair blonde, got rid of the heavy eye makeup. Looked different, maybe. Still pale and small with pink lips like a mouse, but different maybe now. Older, anyway. Mum had wanted to move but Uncle was a shoo-in for foreman. Where would they go? he asked. Anywhere, Mum said. We're staying put, Uncle said.

A door slammed again. The house shook with it.

'Look what *you* done!' Uncle was screaming. 'Look what you made me do!'

Dobbie was wailing, his voice pulsing up and down the thin walls.

'Fuck's sake!' said Mum.

Shona's door popped open.

'It's you he wants,' said Mum.

Dobbie's chubby brown body slid off Mum and thumped onto the purple duvet. He looked sweaty and his nose was running. He was whining still. Shona rolled over and dumbly opened the covers. She held out her arms.

'C'mere,' she said.

Dobbie looked at her with his bulgy dark eyes and crawled in. His cheeks were wet. Shona's head was thuddy.

'Night, Mum,' she said.

Mum left and shut the door.

Dobbie snuggled his little body against hers, wetting her arm with snot.

'Kissy Ma,' said Dobbie and then stuck his thumb back in his mouth. Shona considered his heft, his limbs, his runny nose.

'Good boy,' she said. 'Kissy.'

Bottle on one side, baby on the other, Shona closed her eyes.

The sign was still there, just like on the TV.

JOB PART-TIME ENQUIRE WITHIN.

Shona bit her lip. There was someone inside, doing something behind the counter with their back to the heavy glass door. It had that same stick about it. Needed the little extra nudge to get you through. The beads tinkled; Shona stood just a little way in. The thick, stale smell hung in the air.

'We're closed,' the woman said without turning around. 'Open at ten.'

Sturdy woman, short, with dyed red hair piled up on her head.

'I said we're closed.'

'Hi, Mrs R,' said Shona.

Gil's wife saw Shona then. Took her in from bottom to top, like slitting someone from their chest right up to their nose.

'He's not here,' she said.

Someone had stuck new photos up to show the different things you could get. Shit photos though, bad lighting. The curries looked dark and sludgy, the burgers flat and cold.

'I want my job back,' Shona said. 'I'm good at it.'

'Ha!' Gil's wife said with a snort. She turned away then, to the fryer. Took up a brush and started scrubbing.

Shona rolled off the backpack, pushed up her sleeves. 'I'll take the scraps out the back,' she said. Went straight for the pink bucket.

Four years had passed but her body knew just what to do here. Was itching for it. That strong good feeling. Yank down on the fryer, wrap up the bundles brisk and quick, feel the weight of them hot in your hands as you pass them over.

Shona knew who she was when she was here. Steady, capable, grown up. Gil even let her deal with the dickheads on Friday night. Knew she was tough enough. A few sharp words, a bit of a sneer. She remembered the first time he'd put his big weathered hand on the diamond of her back, just above her bra. He'd left it there long enough for her to know he'd jump in if she needed it.

'You walk over this line, I'll have you arrested,' the wife said.

'I'm a good worker.'

'Get out.' She was holding the scrubber like a knife. Her face was one hard line.

Shona shifted her weight from foot to foot. 'Mum's been laid off. I need a job. You wouldn't even have to train me.'

'No, but I'd have to look at you.'

Shona laughed. Didn't mean to but it slipped out anyway. She peered around past the fryers to the freeze room.

'I told you, he's not here.'

'Just for three months. Then I'll be gone. Wellington. For university.'

'Bully for you. If you think we owe you something you're dead wrong.'

What did Shona think was going to happen? Some kind of Mr Miyagi *Karate Kid* moment? Trade insults with Gil's wife until she cracked and took Shona in? A montage of scrubbing, salting, tossing, frying? Fat little envelope at the end of the week, *a little extra for the kid*?

'No job's going for you. Clear off.'

'Ma! Ma!' Dobbie was jiggling up and down on the pavement outside, his arms raised up above his head like he was on a rollercoaster. 'Ma!'

Shona pushed open the door. 'I told you—stay in the park. Can't I have five minutes to myself?'

'Aw, Ma!' He pawed at the beads, stumbled in. His jandals skidded on the tiles. She grabbed his arm, shook him.

'Do what you're told.'

'Ma!' Dobbie shrugged her off and stuck his finger up his nose.

Mrs R wiped her hands on her smock and came around to get a better look. 'Little fatty, isn't he?'

'Runs in the family,' Shona said.

'I'm hungry,' said Dobbie.

'We're leaving,' said Shona.

'What are you gonna do with him when you're at *university*?' She made the word sound ugly.

'None of your business,' said Shona.

Mrs R rifled around in a box on the counter. 'Here you go,' she said, holding out a Buzz Bar to Dobbie. She made it dance for a moment, the yellow wrapper the same colour as the chip shop's walls. He got shy then, clung to Shona's thigh and hid behind it.

'Go on, pet,' Mrs R said.

Dobbie stuck his thumb in his mouth. Shona couldn't remember whether Mrs R had any kids of her own.

'Go on,' said Shona. 'Take it.' She pushed Dobbie towards the waiting Buzz Bar. He snatched at it and then gave it to Shona to open.

Mrs R was fixing the box so it was straight again. 'They bashed the shit out of him, you know? Put him in hospital.'

'Yeah, saw it on TV.'

'Tanya's big brother and his mates.'

'Oh yeah?'

Shona wondered how good a worker Tanya had been. Skinny little bint. She saw her around school sometimes. Looked permanently startled like someone had just slapped her. Tanya was a fucken thief. Stole Shona's job when Gil got all keyed up and sent her packing. Shona cornered her one day at school, told her to rack off, but Tanya gave it right back.

'Job's mine now. You can't go working when you're up the duff,' Tanya had said, giving a silly smile like she knew all about it.

Gee, big tough Tanya with her brother and his mates. It doesn't count if someone else has to do your dirty work for you.

The difference between someone like Tanya and someone like Shona, Shona thought, was that Shona liked it.

That night in the back of the freeze room she had stood holding one of the kilo bags of chips in her arms like it was a dead man. She knew he was gonna come. He'd followed her in a few days before, made some excuse about the cold, pressed right up against her warm body. So she'd waited. Stood there counting in her head—*one Mississippi, two Mississippi*. Felt her skin turn goosey and blue. On twenty Mississippi, the door creaked and there was a rush of heat from the kitchen on her back. He shut the door behind him. She stood very still.

'My tough little Bunny,' he said, warm beer breath in her ear.

Shona had let her body go lax. Let it melt against his. One leathery finger snaked around, slid across her cheek and into her mouth to suck.

'Bunny, Bunny, Bunny. My little honey,' he said.

And it was true. There was oozing liquid honey running all through her. The loose silky feeling between her legs.

'Is he gonna, you know, die?' said Shona.

Mrs R rubbed at her temples. Looked away.

'Can I've one more?' said Dobbie.

'Just clear off now,' Mrs R said in a quiet voice.

'Can I?' said Dobbie, looking back and forth between them. 'Ma? Can I?'

'What's the word?' said Mrs R.

'Please?' said Dobbie with that gaping look he had on his face sometimes. That look that made you wonder how often he'd fallen over.

'Good boy,' the two of them said at the same time.

Shona and Dobbie sat on the steps of the memorial so Shona could have a smoke. Dobbie tried to drink out of a brown bottle someone had left but Shona snatched it just in time.

'What's uni-verse-city?' said Dobbie.

'It's a big building that looks out over the sea.'

'You gonna go in a boat, Ma?'

'Maybe. Don't tell Mum.'

'Okay,' Dobbie said, digging in the ground with a stick.

Shona looked out at the stubby trees, the flat boxy buildings beyond them. Bit scuzzy. Nothing to do but not a bad town. Stupid TV people getting it all wrong.

'Can I come, Ma? On the boat?'

'Dunno yet, we'll see. C'mere.'

Dobbie chucked the stick away. His smile was broad, his nose snotty. On her lap, he kicked against her shin with his jandal. Kick, kick, kick. Shona pressed him against her. Leaned back. With the other hand she ran her fingers along the stone letters carved into the memorial. The edges and the ridges. The names reached up and up.

It came to her then, the thought she'd been working on all day. Some things can't be undone. Just need to be carried.

VINCENT O'SULLIVAN

Festival Highlight

That dreadful urge, a woman said,
to write, there's so much to write,
but the words aren't there, you
know what it's like? she asks
at a fiction workshop, the suffering
one goes through with that particular

version of distress? Embarrassment
hovers. The writer on stage nods kindly
as a nurse holding high a bottle
for transfusions as you sometimes
see in news from war zones.
She's crying, actually, the woman

who asked the question, a right
spectacle no one likes to say
outright, several writers
already shaping their forms of pity,
possible motives, stories on the make.
As the woman knows, which is why it hurts.

Epiphanies, Half Price

You might not believe this, which is what
I saw, God's truth, in Upland Road.

A significant person walked from a tall
doorway, a lesser person but significant
too in her way, rode his shoulders
with the casual ease of a smoker on a stallion
in that old advertisement, remember,
for Marlboro, in the days of benighted lungs?

And on her handsome shoulders yet another,
the way a Chinese circus arrives in town.
And so on, smaller, small, until a tiny
figure raising one arm as the naked
man on the war memorial raises his
so the sun sits there on a single finger.
The distant highest figure frail as a bat,
its knuckles scorched by the golden hoop
it hangs to. All this in Upland Road.
A bat's wee face at the very rim of the sun.

SUDHA RAO

Watching Ants

She is on her belly.
    A polished floor
        gleams as red ants
            undulate in single file.
                She watches precision, sees blind focus and purpose.
                Hundreds pass.
                  She is vast.
                      She is holding on to a coat tail
and marching, marching, marching. She is now a string across the shiny floor,
hundreds of feet drumming and humming. Blind faith, a fast-paced race across an
endless terrain.
There is no reason to fear, there is no danger.
These are my comrades
        bound for a crack in the wall.
            I am vast, the crack is not, she is back,
                back with legs and arms too few
                      to be an ant. She is on her belly
                        watching.

HARRY RICKETTS

An Afternoon in the Universal Café, Mumbai

Sanjit sweeps each square with care.
Stevie sips tea, *The Awkward Age*.
One for his nob; crib goes on for hours.
Sanjit sweeps each square with care.
India loses to South Africa. Light crumbles blue to grey.
A small girl begs, is shooed away.
Sanjit sweeps each square with care.
Stevie sips tea, *The Awkward Age*.

HARRY RICKETTS

Pink Blanket

There's a multi-coloured 'Happy Birthday'
above the door with balloons.

'Happy 92 today,' I say.
She's sitting in a wheelchair

in a floral dressing-gown,
pink blanket over her knees.

I give her the card, which she opens.
'Lovely,' I think she says. It's rabbits.

I take her vein-mottled hand,
start to tell her about India,

how cows walk at will all over
the street, the road, the motorway.

She starts, one-handed, to fold
and refold the pink blanket,

exposing her bare left knee,
scrutinising it with great attention.

I replace the blanket, try camels,
horses, donkeys, dogs, finally

an old photo of my long-dead father,
taken by her. 'Do you know who

this is?' She shakes her head.
She refolds the pink blanket,

exposes her bare left knee,
gives me a nose-crinkling grin.

JOHN SUMMERS

Pagans

She'll be scrap now, the *Jane Adair*. She was old even then, putt-putting into the bay, towards tin roofs and the blur of bush across the hills. Mrs Waterson was the only other passenger and, as we came closer, I could see her family on the jetty. Her father and the sister who'd never married, each hugging themselves against the breeze. Dad once dismissed the whole clan as having 'no hope of a chin between them', and a look over this lot didn't offer much ammunition for argument. But it was Grandad I was looking for, and for a moment I panicked, thinking he hadn't remembered or that maybe he was ill. I forgot the seasickness that had kept me bloated for most of the trip. And then I spotted him, further back behind the rest, a tall old man leaning against the railing in his Sunday suit, the only one who didn't seem anxious to get home.

He waited till Captain Hobb lifted our bags out and the others had hurried away before he stepped forward. 'What do you know?' he said.

I hated this question—I never knew what the right answer might be. 'Not too much,' I said, what I always said, and then, 'Just school.'

'And how's that going for you this year?'

'Not very well. I don't think I'll get proficiency.'

'If I knew what that was I might be concerned,' he said as we started to walk away from the wharf, stopping to retrieve a cigar from his coat pocket. 'Then again, I might not.'

I laughed at that. A bit of a splutter, because it was so different from what other adults would say. But he looked serious, and he took a long pull on the cigar.

'Tell your father to pinch me some better cigars next time, or even better some good pipe tobacco. Surely those Americans wouldn't notice a few tins in the unloading.'

'I'll tell him.'

'School is a funny business. The important thing is to do your best …' He took another long pull, '… to forget everything they tell you once you leave.'

I laughed again and this time he smiled back. We stepped off the main street, the only one you'd call a street really, just a stretch long enough for the church, pub, schoolhouse and store. And now that we'd passed all that and begun on the dirt path up through the white pines and on to his house, he talked about his theories.

They were based on all the books he'd read, ideas he must have formulated and revised during his hours of work, out alone in the fields or milking shed. There were better ways to understand the past than through dates and events, he said. It revolved like the elliptical cogs you sometimes saw in machinery. There were distinct points and lean periods in between. You could be sure that things would come back to us—a war as big as the last would be upon us in a hundred years or so. I'd heard some of this before and although I might not have followed his meaning, I could tell these theories were important to him and he wanted me to share them. He mentioned his books as if I might be familiar with the contents. 'Ignore me,' he said, 'if you've already read Major Douglas.'

I imagined he spoke to me no differently to the way he might to someone much older, someone official and important—a judge or a member of parliament. And so I nodded along, asking, 'Why is that?' or 'Do you think that many others think this too?' Questions that would show I was listening but not reveal my ignorance. But after a while he didn't wait for the questions. He talked on all the same, telling me a long story involving Napoleon and some Russian, and I could see a big white fleck stuck to his lip. His mouth moved too fast; his lips were too dry and never touched together properly to shift it.

Seeing this saddened me, I have to say. It was proof of something I had hoped to be wrong about, a reminder of what Dad had said after coming to the bay several months back and finding time to chat with some men in the pub and at Mullan's store. Grandad didn't do justice to his land, they'd told him. He left both planting and harvest until almost too late. Somehow I'd known these theories were part of the picture—his strong views and book reading would be considered weaknesses by those men. Dad wasn't shy about criticising him either. Any mention of Grandad and he would shake his head sadly. 'A poor, poor farmer, that man.' He spoke in the same dry way he had summed up the Watersons. There was no pleasure in his saying it, this meant, but he had a duty to do so.

Margaret Jamieson called good evening from the kitchen, coming to the hall only once we'd placed my bag in Uncle Don's old room. Really she was Margaret Cassell then, but I would always think of her as a Jamieson. A skinny lady, almost as tall as Grandad. Everyone wondered why she had married so old, but most of all they wondered why she married him, a man so much older. Her hair was still dark except for the odd grey streak, her face lined but still firm. All I knew was—again it was what I'd been told—that he'd been visiting her family in Beech Bay, the next one over, for years. They sold seed and grain, and Grandad had been great friends with her father before he'd died. One day, Dad said, he'd come back from Beech Bay engaged. He went back a few months later and they were married.

'So you'll be our guest for a bit,' she said, and that was almost the only sound she made, but for tuts at some of the more outrageous comments from Grandad as we ate our chops. Christmas was a pagan festival long before it belonged to the Christians, he said. There are some people whose hair bleeds if not treated carefully before it's cut. It was when he passed me the butter dish, saying, 'The Chinese are the world's best farmers,' that she put down her knife with a clank.

'Well,' she said, 'if that's correct than perhaps we should welcome some Chinamen here, on this very farm.'

He looked at her, his eyebrows high, before turning to smile at me. 'A fine idea, but we have Clem here to help us whip this farm into shape.'

And with that he went back to his talk and her to her tuts until it came time for them both to wish me goodnight.

We weren't allowed to speak of Uncle Don at home but I thought about him that night as I waited for sleep, listening to the cicadas whirring away. I was lying in his bed after all, the same sheets he had once lain in. They even had a military feel to them—stiff and sandpapery and the colour gone a bit khaki, but that made no sense. Probably it was because they'd been unused for so long. They hadn't had a chance to wear soft. Was it true, I wondered, what they said about there being nothing left to bury? It was a strange thing to have two tombstones—the one there next to Grandma's in the bay graveyard and another in France—but no body under either.

Grandad was quieter at breakfast, winking as he spooned extra sugar onto my porridge. But it was Margaret Jamieson who had a real way of being quiet. It was a silence that was a presence, somehow. You felt that sooner or later she would shout something, and her quiet made everything else loud. The scrape of a spoon against a plate was a screech, the things Grandad said were shouts.

'We'll be making fenceposts from that tōtara,' he told her. 'I've been waiting for a man who can swing an axe and just now I have one.'

He must have lined up help, I thought, and then understood it was me he was talking about, although he'd never seen me even pick up an axe before.

It was early but already he had been out to milk. I was a bit miffed about that. I was there to help, and I knew what Dad would say if he found out I had slept while an old man worked.

'It's your holiday,' was what Grandad had said. 'We can't have you working every minute.' And so, still feeling the need to contribute, I gulped my porridge so that I might be ready.

'Where are you going to fence?'

'We have some land back there that's still bush. I'd like to keep stock out of it. Every day in this bay somebody makes grazing land, but I don't see anyone making more bush as beautiful as this. A chapel is what it is, the beams made by nature itself.'

'Pagans again,' Margaret said, as if repeating her words to someone hard of hearing.

Grandad brightened. 'A pagan I am, then. But one who must go to work.'

He had cut the tōtara two summers back, and it lay in the tall grass of the back paddock. He walked around it a couple of times, rubbing his hands together. I followed without knowing what he was up to, and almost walked into him when he suddenly came to a stop.

'I've forgotten the tools,' he suddenly said, though he had brought a maul and wedges, and I held an axe. Even stranger, he carried the maul as he walked back towards the shed, muttering to himself until he turned, half realising, and saw that my mouth hung open.

'You take a good look at where we might cut and split it for the most posts.'

I did as I was asked, using my hands to trace out the butts of fenceposts on the sawn end. First I counted twenty posts, but by the time I finished I couldn't see those imaginary splits and cuts, and I counted again to get fifteen. My third count gave me twenty-three, and I decided not to count again until I knew he was approaching, so I wouldn't need to hold the result in my head for quite so long. I hoisted myself onto a trunk to sit and wait, and peered into the bush. It was messy, a dark scramble of shrubs and gnarled trunks. Two waxeyes flitted in and out of the shadows like thieves.

'How are we?' He was almost back, carrying two slashers. 'Plenty of posts in it?'

My mouth fluttered. I hadn't had time for my recount. 'Yes,' I said.

'Good, good. It'll wait, though. Let's clear out this mess, shall we?'

He walked into that gloom, crunching down a dried-out fern and sending those waxeyes away. He threw one of the slashers down near my feet, and arranged his hands on the second, swinging it into a young beech. There was a flash of its white flesh and it tilted to one side.

'Cut what you can and leave the big trunks for later,' he said.

I slid off the trunk to pick up the tool. 'Isn't this the bit of bush you wanted to keep?'

'Oh it was. But you've no doubt heard how much they're paying for cocksfoot seed.'

It was the sort of thing Dad would say. He loved to speak of prices and seasons. Practical, certain things that made him practical and certain. But it was odd coming from Grandad. He made the price of seed sound like a rumour he was embarrassed to be spreading.

'You see, this paddock—if we planted it from the gully in cocksfoot it could carry on right through here.' He nodded at the bush. 'That would make for a nice clean harvest of the stuff.'

'I thought ...' I began, but I saw that he was fiddling with the end of his slasher, anticipating the question with an anxious look, and so instead I said, 'Be good to clear it out.'

Together the two of us walked at the bush swinging, battering branches and shrubs so they hung over limp, exposing damp leaves to raw sunlight for the first time.

That job would take most of my week there. At lunch, Margaret Jamieson came down with a basket of bread, a couple of cold chops each and a billy of tea. 'The likely lads,' she said each time, brighter as the days went on and the bush became brighter too, just big trees standing proud with all that cleared space around them.

She was more inclined to smile than tut at Grandad by then, pleased with our work. What she didn't see was the way we lingered, lying on the grass long after she left, or Grandad stopping often to smoke. He'd ask me to stop too. 'There's no great hurry I can see,' he'd say, and again remind me that it was my holiday from school.

He gave me an even longer lecture on this theme when he learned I was working at it in the early mornings when he was milking. 'You should be having a more restful time of it. Read a book or go for a walk instead. You won't get much chance for that when you're older.'

In truth, I would have preferred to go for a walk—the bay was beautiful. It had its own sharp light, singling out every leaf, every feather on a bellbird's coat. Dusty roads led down to the surf. But more than anything I wanted to help—and to show him. I worked just as hard when no one was there to see me, at least I had thought no one was there. On one of those mornings Margaret Jamieson came down early, surprising me as I dragged out a branch.

'I thought you might like something as a snack,' she said, and she held out a bowl covered with a tea-towel. 'It's not much, just a couple of scones.'

'Sounds good to me,' I said, and put down the branch.

'Well, we have to show our thanks however we can. We're very grateful for the help you've given him. It's a great thing you're doing here.' She looked at what we'd cut away. 'Opening all this up so we can get things going with the farm.'

I was a little embarrassed. 'It's not much,' is all I said, and she went, leaving the bowl on the ground. A funny lady, I thought as I chewed on my scone. You'd think she was the farmer herself, showing such interest. I believed then that women were apart from such things; that my mother's silence during Dad's talk of work and money proved a lack of interest, even though I had seen how mad he got when questioned.

With these views already formed and Margaret Jamieson thus confirmed as odd, I began to wonder again about their courtship in Beech Bay. How did you get a woman to like you? Probably Grandad sat at the Jamiesons' table telling stories to them all. Margaret shy but giggling, sometimes meeting his eyes. Surely that's how it would have been.

No doubt I thought that because of all the stories he was telling me. As well as his usual subjects, the world's great civilisations and the ways of the American Indians, he had begun to yarn about himself, about being my age. As he talked he waved his cigar around—these days it just takes the slightest whiff of rolled tobacco, I might be hurrying along a street in town and suddenly I'm back at Grandad's. Everything is forgotten and instead I'm in the sun on the edge of the bush, my legs stretched out and a slasher lying beside me, listening to him talk.

'Education was quite the commodity then,' he said. 'Oh yes, I would have given anything to carry on and study. But we had this farm of course, and no money to farm it. With sisters, there was nothing to be done but make me work.'

'Where did you learn all these things then?'

'Well, I thought if I'm not going to get a proper education, I'll fill in what I can myself and that's when I started at being a great book reader. I read anything I could get my hands on. And you know what?'

'What?'

'Since then I've met these fellows who had all the schooling I missed, and they don't know any of what I've read. What they do know you could write on the edge of that slasher blade.' He laughed at that, before furrowing his brow and turning to me. 'You're a smart one,' he said, 'and that's the truth.' He chewed at his lip as if he wanted to say more, but instead went back to work.

Grandad and Margaret came to the wharf when it was time to see me off. He insisted on carrying my bag, and she wore Sunday clothes, her blouse boiled white.

'You come back any time you want,' she said.

'I will.'

'Yes,' he said, 'and the next time you see me I'll be King Cocksfoot. We'll have the stuff planted from windowsill to road edge.'

Margaret swatted at him, laughing, and he gave me a wink she couldn't see.

'Good man,' he said, his voice solemn. 'Good man.' He shook my hand.

I went back to school, the whole class in a panic as our proficiency tests approached. Mr Mihinnick believed he had some insight into the exam content that year, and so he had us chanting an even narrower range of facts and figures than usual. I filled my head with these scraps of information. Layers on layers like compost. As a result, when I came to sit my paper I could lift out the odd fact—the Battle of Hastings in 1066, Drake embarking in 1577—but the rest was muddled, harder to separate. It was only just a fail, they said, but it meant the end of schooling for me.

I expected hell from Dad but he wasn't fazed. He didn't get angry, he didn't mind at all. 'You've had more than enough school,' he said, and he had me painting the fowlhouse, dunny and back fence with some paint he got from the docks—special thick stuff that was hard to get off your hands. I was to do this till he found work for me.

I've never been afraid of work, but I worried what he would come up with— on more than one occasion he mentioned the way men at the docks had started out shovelling coal or guano. I fancied myself more in a trade, maybe fitting and turning, something where you got to think about things as you worked, rather than simply rushing to finish while a boss watched you.

Mum kept silent on my results. She was a quiet woman generally, and saying something like 'You'll be finished the hen-house soon' or 'Lunch is on the table' was about the height of our conversation. Then again, having spent those days with Grandad, and knowing the way Dad spoke his mind, I could see how she might have thought there was enough talk going on already.

And then one day I came in from painting, my hands tender from turpentine, to find her sitting in the corner chair. It was her knitting chair because it didn't have arms, but she was still. Dad came into the room—home early. 'I have some news for you,' he said.

I closed the door behind me. So here it was. He'd found me a job.

'Some might say bad news, but information is just information in my view, and I won't attempt to pass a judgement on the necessary matters of life.' He paused and looked at me. He licked his lips.

It had to be the docks, or something worse. I waited for it, feeling his eyes on me.

'Tell him!' Mum shouted all of a sudden, and both of us looked to her in surprise. Dad began to turn around, to address this interruption, but hesitated.

'Just tell him,' she said.

'Your grandfather is dead. On Sunday. He keeled over while trying to fell a tree. Why he was attempting that in the midday sun I don't know. He died that night. Heart trouble, they tell us.'

I looked up to the ceiling, the long branching crack in the plaster. I looked at my shoes, at the table, anywhere but at Dad. I didn't want him to see tears. I looked at Mum but her eyes were fixed on a point on the floor.

'I have no doubt he's left an untidy state of affairs,' Dad continued. 'Both the land and the business lacked the attention they needed.'

Most of the bay turned out for the funeral, and Mum, Dad and I were there. It was the first I had ever been to—I was too young to have been at Grandma's or even the service they held for Don. The minister read at length from the Bible, and except for the name on the tombstone it could have been anyone they were burying.

Mum and Dad went home, leaving me in the bay for a few more days. It was agreed that I'd stay to do the milking and other necessary jobs till they decided what would happen with the farm.

At first, when we arrived in the *Jane Adair* again, I found myself looking out for him, expecting him at the wharf just like before, but as I started to do those chores, it felt as if he'd never been, as if it was just daydreams I'd had, and all this—doing the milking, the cows unused to me, kicking and shunting—this was the reality.

I wasn't alone. I was in Don's room again, and Margaret Jamieson was still there. I thought that would be uncomfortable—I had never been alone with her before—but she treated me pretty well.

'If there's something you like to eat you let me know,' she said on the first night that it was just me and her. 'It's only a simple kitchen but I can always rustle something up.'

'This all tastes good to me.' She was a better cook than Mum, dishing up more meat than we ever ate back home—chops that were soft through but with a coating of crisped and salted flour. Potatoes that had the rich taste of the lamb.

Every night I came in to a meal like that, puddings each time, and praise for my work too.

'You've done a wonderful job with those fences,' she said after I fixed one, the first time I used strainers. It was embarrassing—I was no real farmhand but I still liked to hear it. What I really wished she'd say though was something about Grandad, something to show she missed him and to prove he'd been there. I began to look for a sign of it, and instead started to see the way her face was set, the way she gazed past me, smiling if I caught her eye and offering some comment about puddings or fences but nothing more. She was hardened, off elsewhere, and after first feeling awkward, so conscious of this other person being there, it soon got to be that I was lonely.

I finished the milking early one morning and snuck down to the gully where he and I had cleared away that bush. There I thought I would find some proof.

The tōtara log still lay there, the grass longer around it. And there were plenty of tōtara and other trees still standing in the space he had wanted cleared—cutting them down was to be the next job. The ground around those trees wasn't quite bare, just messy and trampled. Chopped and hacked scrub was heaped up in places, and in the full sun the leafmould was dry. I imagined it smelt like tobacco so I sat down, leaning my back against one rough trunk, closed my eyes and sniffed.

I cried a little then, and wondered why he couldn't have just left it and gone without the cocksfoot. It was because of people like Dad and Margaret. They weren't happy for Grandad not to do things they would have done, even if it was his land. I was sure she had goaded him to it, out of greed and worry about what the neighbours thought. And where had it got her? He was gone because of it. She'd be gone soon and so would I, off to shovel bird shit all day with Dad nearby.

That evening was like most. She was impressed that I had moved some cows from one paddock to another, but otherwise we sat there quietly, until she took my plate away and came back with a bowl of rice pudding, steaming hot. 'Your favourite, isn't it?'

'Yes.'

'Don't say I don't look after my workers.'

'Oh no, I wouldn't say that. It's all … very nice.' I didn't know quite how to respond—she hadn't spoken to me like that, in a joking way, before.

'And all those jobs, you're very good at them. You must enjoy working out there on this farm.'

'I do,' I said, realising that she was right. I did like the work. I got to learn things as I went, without Dad or Mr Mihinnick leaning over me all the time. Instead it was just her at the end of the day saying I'd done a fine job. And there was the bay itself, its trees and crisp air. Back home, the boats meant soot was everywhere; on a still day you breathed it in.

'I understand your father is coming tomorrow to take you home, and to make arrangements with me about this old place. Really though, I'd like to stay here. You can understand that.'

She looked at me hard, and I nodded before glancing down at my rice pudding. A skin had started to form on top.

'I thought you would. You'd like to stay yourself, I imagine? You could work here, just like your grandfather did, and make a real go of this place. Plant that cocksfoot?'

'I'd like that, but Dad's finding work for me in town.'

'Let me talk to him about that. We can tell him that this is your grandfather's farm and it's your right to stay, follow in his footsteps.'

'I don't know. I don't think he'll like that,' I said. She had begun to scare me a little, with her fixed way of looking and this talk of Grandad after all those days of silence. I felt unprepared, believing there was more being discussed than I knew. 'I think I better go with Dad.'

When I looked up she was no longer smiling. 'And what happens to me then?' she said. 'What will I do?'

She spoke quickly, more quietly than before, with one hand pressed so hard on the table that it had gone bloodless. 'And you'll just sail out of here.'

'Maybe Dad can help,' I said.

'Your father?' she scoffed. 'A lot he'll do for me.' She shook her head slowly. We were both staring at the pudding now.

I worried she would cry, and then what would I do? This was a conversation she should be having with Mum or Dad, not me. I desperately wanted to go back to the polite, lonely way that it had been before.

'Thanks for tea,' I said.

She looked at me and frowned. Then she got up from the table and walked out of the room, down to her bedroom at the other end of the house.

The next morning my breakfast was on the table and she was nowhere to be seen. It was a relief. I wouldn't have known what to say. As I milked, I went over it again and again: her anger and my idiotic reply. I winced each time and I revised my response, too, so that it became more sympathetic as the morning went on.

I needed to say something. And so, when I saw Dad walking up the path, waving to me as I shifted cattle from one paddock to another (I wasn't sure how necessary this was, but knew it was something farmers did regularly), I shouted to him to wait.

Running over, I arrived breathless to find him irritated at me interrupting his business. My thoughts came out stunted, hints instead of points. 'I can stay here longer and help,' I said. 'I've got the hang of things.'

'No need, Clem. I've arranged things.'

'I can stay,' I said.

He narrowed his eyes. 'Did she put you up to this?'

'What?'

He looked at the house. Margaret was at the door. Tired, and looking older than she ever had before. Dad muttered something; I caught the words 'old bitch'.

He pushed past me and carried on towards the house. Margaret went inside and he followed.

Neither looked back at me, and Dad closed the door. I would hear him begin to shout soon, but until then it was quiet. The only sounds were the cows chewing away, mooing to themselves, oblivious. The bay was theirs.

DOC DRUMHELLER

No Vacancy

The body is a hotel for the soul.
Neon vacancy signs light up America.

I have learned more about myself behind
closed doors of these temporary domiciles

than all I have sensed or sensationalised
to make the personal universal

through the anonymity of travel
humbled by the quiet moments of solitude.

Where I found the greatest gift I have received
was to forgive those who had hurt me the most.

As expressed in the final analysis
by the holy Saint Mother Teresa

forgive them anyway, be kind anyway,
it was never between you and them anyway.

BRIAR WOOD

Celebrants

Welcoming manuhiri at Waimate North,
Jill was a flight attendant
in a previous life, now minds the desk
and drives tourists all over Northland.

Distantly related to Kawiti,
a man of action, yet her preserve
is to find an apposite speech
for each unique occasion.

We're seated on a bench looking out
across the lawn where Darwin
played cricket one Christmas,
then slipped away to Waiomio.

After Tahiti, New Zealand proved
a disappointment to him, lacking
in 'charming simplicity'. And soap.
Some customs frightened him—

and cruel ideas later dispersed
by association with his writing
are rejected in his preference
for the Christian life of the mission.

Religious crazies flourished—such as
the man who shot Rev. Yate's
horse—which had to take the blame
for his sex life. The private door

to his room let lovers in, still there.
A fence survives the marauding
armies and firewood requirements.
From Cook's Lane goods were carted

to Kerikeri, Paihia and back again.
We identify each tree—
planted carefully for future company
under the guidance of watchful iwi—

an immense tōtara, handsome kauri,
a male and female of the variety,
cloudy magnolia, oak, pūriri, rimu,
hoping humans can age as bravely.

C.A.J. WILLIAMS

Tohunga Suppression Act 1907

We sat in a silent circle. A
perfect round circle. At
a breath one by one
we read a sentence then
a paragraph of an English-
speaking newspaper. And
learned of the medicine-
men of the Dakota. The
reservations and deprivation. The
cold and starvation. The
absence of movement. The
fractured kin spread like
flung knuckle-bones. Women
and children deserted mid-
prairie. The lost seasonal
hunting. Every weekday
morning children instructed
to dress for school. We are
expected to read paper-law. And
write our whakapapa lines on
wallpaper off-cuts. For
convenience.

[Repealed 1962]

JILLIAN SULLIVAN

Release

Her father dies the fastest she's seen anyone die. Not drawn out with fever the way her mother suffered after the voyage on the *Strathallan*. And not with infection the way her husband Peter perished on the farm.

'I think I'll go now,' her father said, and before Cassie could finish saying 'I beg your pardon, Father?' he slumped to the breakfast table and was still. Just like that his rule of her was over. She sat in her chair opposite him, the hard oak at her back. Above her the weight and silence of the rooms. A log shifting in the fireplace near her, the *pphtt* of sparks as if a wind had disturbed them.

Outside the window, the width and height of the Old Man Range, the early light showing the folds and crevasses and slopes. Even as she watches, the sun goes out, the clouds settle thickly on the fissures of hill and the temperature in the room lowers. Her ankles chill and her feet on the cold stone floor and her wrists and her cheeks. Winter is upon them, though her father, his cheek resting on the white tablecloth, has no need of seasons, nor the relief from them.

'You'll be all right now, Father,' she says. The kindest words she can muster. At a patter of feet in the hall she calls out.

'Charlie.'

Her father had been averse to suitors. The only chance she had to be wooed was the one time her father was sick—upstairs and waiting for his rum and lemon. Peter asked her father, with whisky and a whole mutton for the table. When he said no, they married anyway. Peter took her back to Mulvaney Station, to the yellow crocheted counterpane and fine lace at the window. Six months they had, before he broke his leg, and the season of loss began.

Not all loss. Charlie was born the day after the death. The snow was lovely on the range, the sun white and sheeny on the slopes. She held her baby up to the window, twiggy body wrapped in woven blanket, and promised that when the sun had melted all the white back to golden grass they would walk up there and look out over the brown hills and turquoise river. They would breathe deep in that air the snow had left behind, and all that was good and true would come to them in time.

The miner arrives the day after her father's funeral, the door held against a bluster of snow. It's as if Peter has walked back into her life. She almost drops the pot roast on the way to table three.

'Excuse me, Ma'am, do you have a bed for the night?'

Her father's room is empty. The bed stripped, the window open all day while clouds swirled and bundled closer and snow began to drift down, soft pennies of it, until by dusk the sky had become a blur.

The man holds his hat, a great bush of black curls, though Peter was fair, but tall like him, slim. She flinches at the wildness of her thoughts.

'There's my father's old room. I can make arrangements shortly. It's not a night for a tent.'

'No, but there are plenty out there,' says the man. 'And I'll be joining them soon enough.'

She ladles a bowl of thick bean soup, slices the crust off a new loaf and takes the food through to the parlour. Charlie is beside him, three-year-old legs next to the long thighs.

'He says he'll take us up to the hills, Mum, and the crunchy little streams.'

'I do not know you,' she says. She places the bowl by the fire.

'My name is—'

'And I'll thank you not to tempt my son.'

'Peter Earl.'

'Up to the hills, Mum.'

Even his name the same. Her fingers are warm from the bowl, her cheeks flamed by the fire. Yet for a moment she is stooped again on the verandah, pain drawing her down to a hollow in her spine. Her husband on the bed inside, his eyes closed under a soft dark cloth. How she'd fought to keep his body there for this moment, when their son would emerge.

'Forgive me, Ma'am.'

The ranges would be there, rising up from paddocks through tussock lands and gullies and the wild herbs blazing, and up into the blueness of air.

'For the imposition.'

And she does.

PHILIP ARMSTRONG

Obiter Dicta

1. Voccus
My uncle liked to cheat at Scrabble
using navy slang like *voccus*
which he reckoned was the crud that ends up
in the bilge: clots of rust, knotted mats
of rope-hair, curdled paint, decaying rats,
sump oil grounds and salty slurry.
We never found it in the dictionary.

He'd served in the British Pacific Fleet and said
what scared them most were US battleships:
if one appeared to port they turned to starboard.
One night on middle watch an officer
told him that right here, in the Mariana
Trench, lay Royal Navy ships sunk
by the itchy-trigger-fingered Yanks.

In the '70s his daughter, just sixteen, fell
pregnant. He threw her out.
They reconciled in time and in the end
she nursed him as he dropped into dementia,
with her grown-up daughter helping,
laughing at the words not found in
dictionaries that sloshed up out of him.

2. Going to a Funeral
My father goes ahead, relinquishing
his pen, his house keys and his old man's
key-pad phone. He stands before the gate,

then shuffles through and makes the siren sing,
forgetting what he always keeps at hand,
coiled in his coin pocket: rosary beads.
Preparing for takeoff he watches and waits
as carry-ons cram into overhead bins,
and takes from his briefcase a book: a breviary,
my sidelong squint corroborates.
Impeccably, implausibly, my own read's
Doctor Faustus. Divinity, adieu!
'Tis magic, magic that hath ravished me.
Reluctantly the flesh accelerates.

MEGAN KITCHING

On Hume's Table

I was writing on Mr. Hume's table.—Rousseau

David Hume is thinking, 'This very table.'
This table here, can't you perceive how very
it is? How square in its four-footed proof
of things, how they bed in existence,
this table, 'which we see white,
and which we feel hard'. I like

to peer through the words at him,
this philosopher, whom we see white,
prodding a finger just to check.
'The paper, on which I write at present,'
his pen scratches, 'is beyond my hand.'
And whoomph: time's very
edifice collapses
none of it has happened
and some atoms we breathe
are back in the body
of a man who sits
at a window, presently
casting his eye like an angler's hook
over the 'great extent of fields and buildings'
the chamber, the walls,
his cramped hand
drawing the ink
across the paper
on the table.

ROSE WHITAU

I, Tambour

My belly is a drumhead, taut
ma petite joueuse de tambour, untaught
her soft bones first bubbled ghost notes
pianissimo
flam tap
flam paradiddle
         popcorn popping on aluminium foil, on paper

She grew by licks,
a quick riff, a quiet ruff
uneven, yes
odd, yes
      but always here, or here, or here
ma petite percussionniste, her throne at Omphalos,
the centre of the world

Now, she,
twenty-seven weeks,
chops her beat spang-a-lang, rolling
                buzz, crush, and press
multiple bounce stroke, strike, struck—blistering
phrasing   everywhere
my boomwhacking bongocera
I am glockenspiel, xylophone, mummy marimba

silence

        I sip tea

Boom! She finds the foot pedal
fortissimo
I wait for the beats I find missing
?like jazz
like space on the page
like her dad's mind, when busy,
              leaves sentences unstrung,
           dangling autumnal,
  phrasing   everywhere

I imagine her poised,
sticks raised
              to catch his beat, to jam

AIWA POOAMORN

A Thai-Chinese Stay-at-Home Mother Gets Political

I got politely kicked out
of the meet-the-candidates event
on account of my crying swearing baby
disrupting speeches
a small crowded room
of angry shushing

Phil Twyford was there
he helped me get the red pram
out of the tiny doorway
I couldn't quite find the right moment
to make him apologise
for scapegoating investors
with Chinese-sounding names
snapping turtles
gobbling up houses
hard-working Kiwis
don't stand a chance
against the Yellow Peril

Phil declined to apologise
he insists he's not racist
it's just the numbers talking

Fuck you Phil and your lousy maths

My Pākehā father-in-law asks me
why are you so angry

you're not even Chinese
you were born in Thailand
you have a Thai passport
you're Thai

I'm as Thai as Pad Thai noodles
invented to be the national dish
by military dictator Phibun
when actually it's quite Chinese
all to create the myth
of a homogeneous monoculture
Thailand the land of smiles
pledge allegiance to
chaat (the Thai nation state)
satsana (the Buddhist religion)
phramahakesat (the demi-god King)

Change your Fb profile to black and white
show your sincere sadness
for the death of the rainmaker
stray dog-loving King
whose tacit approval
allowed the massacre of students
branded communists and enemies of Thainess
for rallying against the return
of exiled military dictator Thanom
dressed in a saffron robe
under the 50-metre-high golden chedi
of Wat Bowonniwet the royal monastery

In Thammasat University
6 October 1976
some hung from trees and beaten
others set afire as the crowd looks on
smiles on their faces

female students raped alive and dead
by the police and military

The Thai nation does not mourn for them
in our collective amnesia
we are too busy admiring
the hot young princess
leading her 77-horse cavalry
to enshrine the royal ashes of our father

He sleeps on a gilded sandalwood pyre
blessed with holy coconut water
awaiting to be carried off to Mount Meru
centre of the Hindu Buddhist universe
in a red gold 42-tonne great victory chariot

while I priestess glide
through Auckland airport
a red pram to part a sea of apsaras
small breasts sway
as white supremacists chant
go home

I say

I am

JILLY O'BRIEN

Dunedin Winter

Socks over shoes

Black ice in the hill suburbs

Full kids or warm ones?

JUSTIN SPIERS

Uneasy Listening

On 16 June 2017 the Dunedin central business district was closed down by a poem. It was titled 'StreetNOISE' and was found attached to a building on Moray Place. The police flew an explosive ordnance bomb disposal unit by helicopter to the scene of the poem to perform a controlled disposal.

Charges laid against its author, however, were promptly dismissed in court, leaving police hands razed.

This series of images offers a glimpse into the world of the man responsible for perplexing the Dunedin police with poetry: artist and musician L.$.D Fundraiser.

1. Untitled
2. Poem Concealed in an Evidence Bag
3. Police Brutality is Alive and Kicking in Dunedin
4. Dene
5. The Economy of Law
6. Nothing Pudding
7. In the Kitchen of L.$.D Fundraiser
8. Nohwere

Spiers and his musician subject together toy with the imaginative projection and creation of identity. This portrait might promise intimacy and psychological revelation of the person behind a notorious (misspelt) publicity stunt—yet it reveals a man in a tatty, comic mask who at one glance has the sadness of clowns, at another, their creepiness. The series has a documentary realism and crispness, yet it leaves us asking what is the musician's private persona?

Shots of a cassette and poster collection suggest analogue museum; clinging to the values of a pre-digital age; increasing obsolescence: the struggle to keep upgrading technology, keep employed, creative, productive, fed and housed. When we see the straitened context behind the musical passion, this composite portrait builds a troubling sense of the sacrifices behind the art.
—Emma Neale

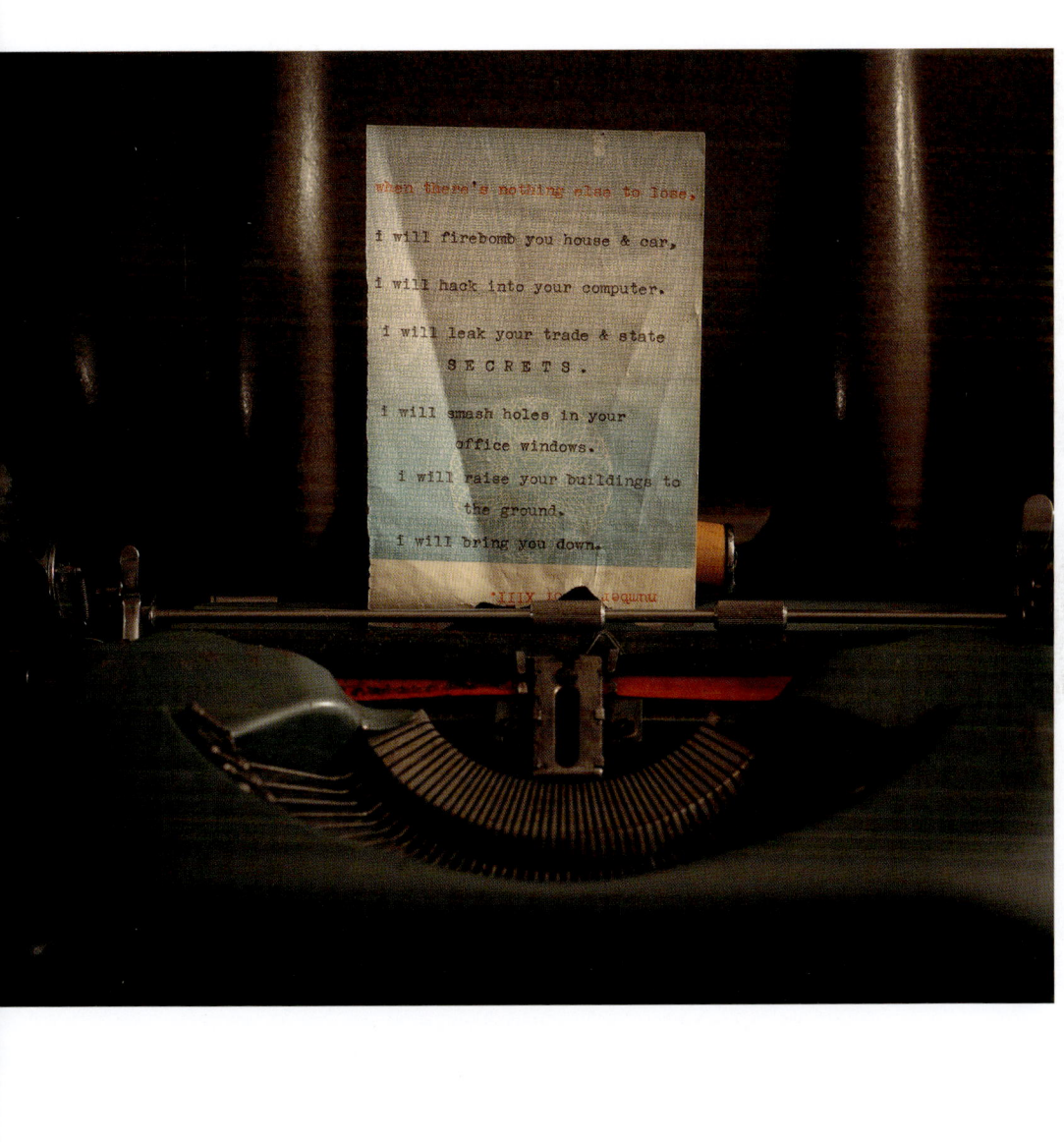

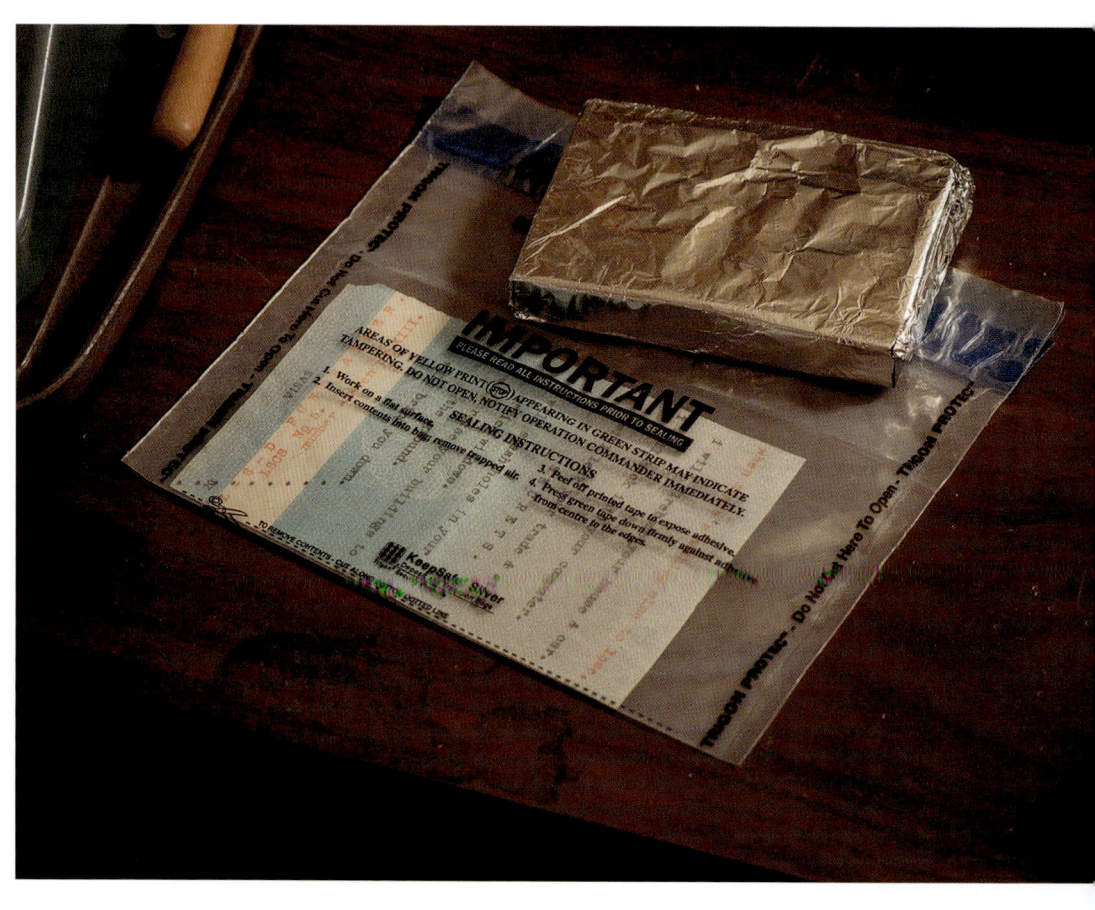

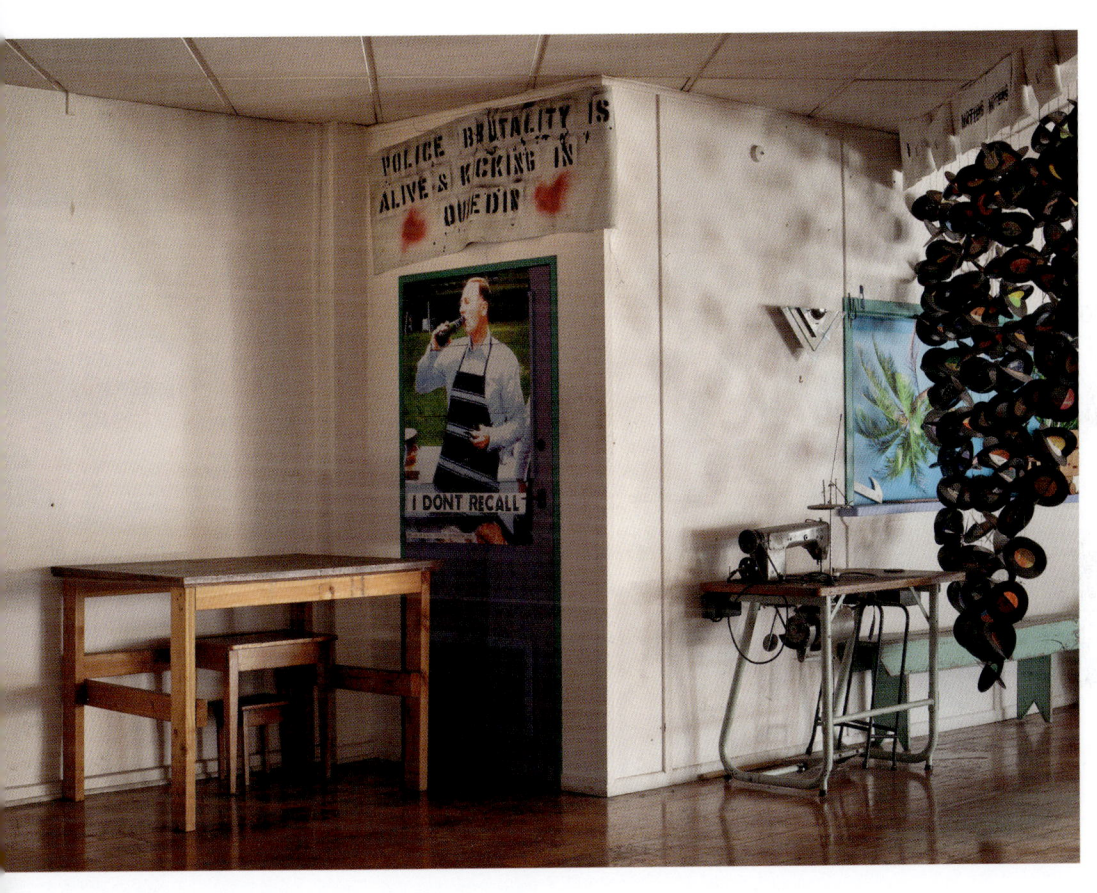

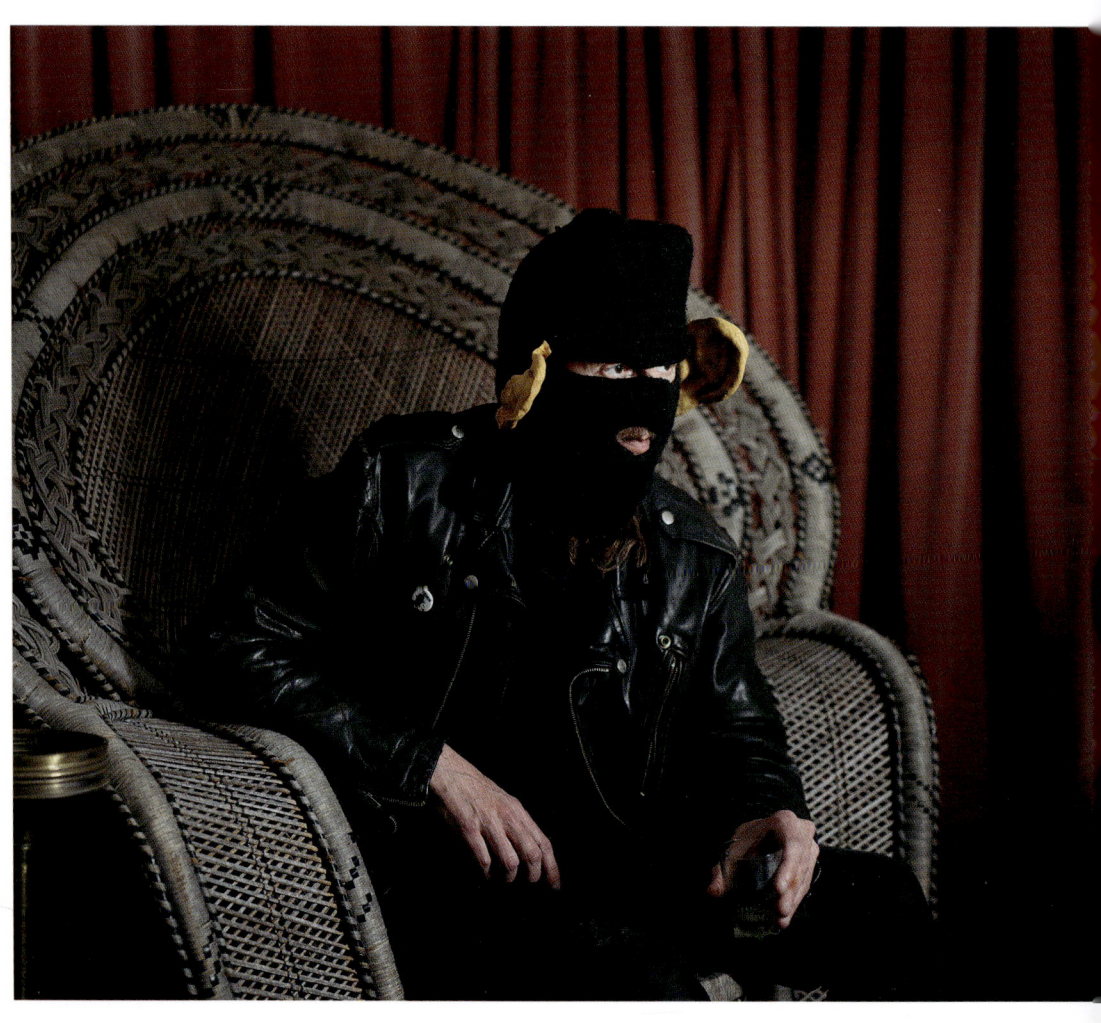

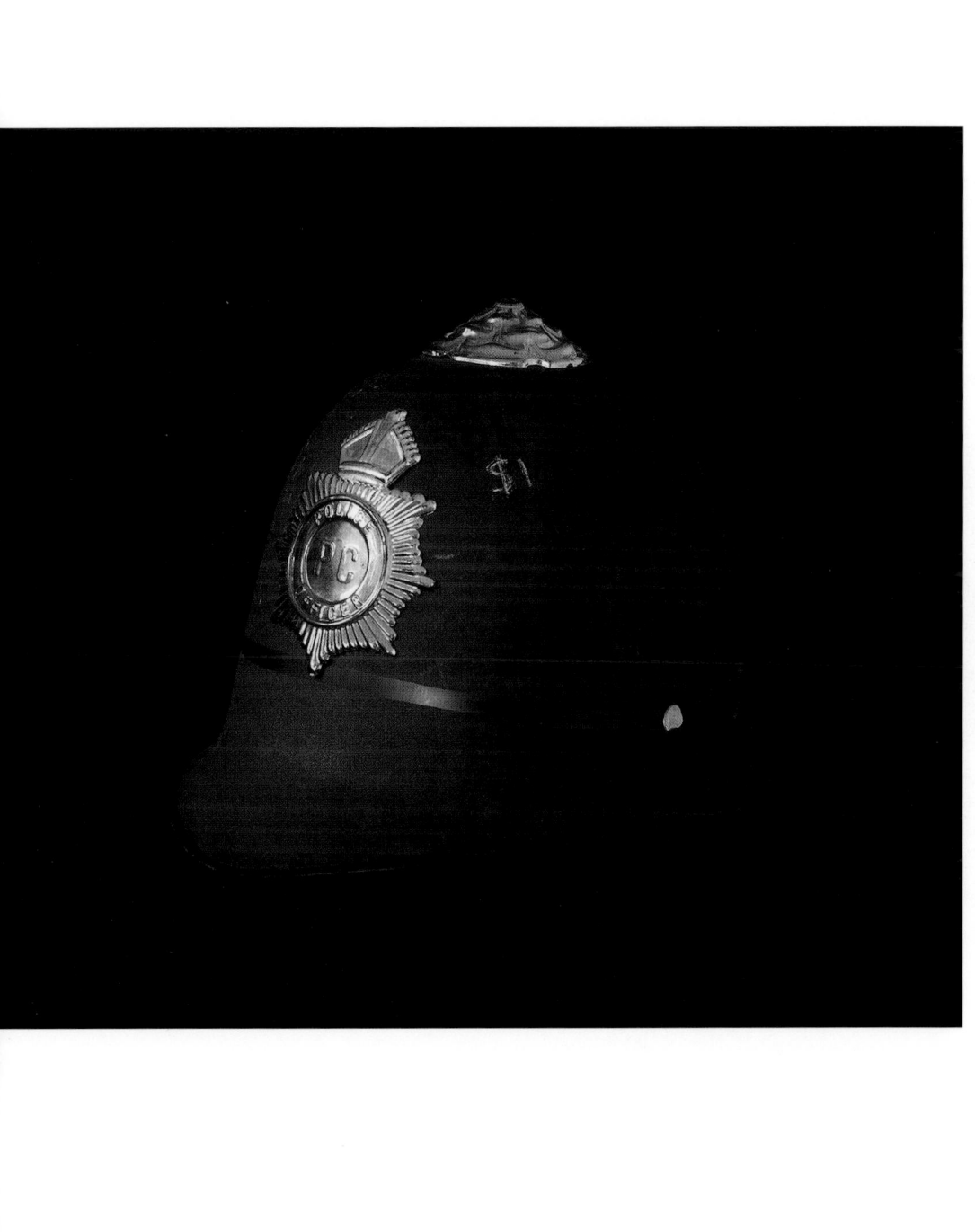

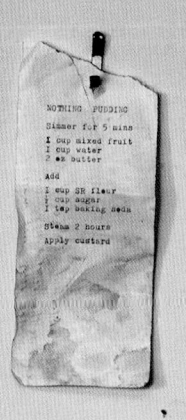

NOTHING PUDDING

Simmer for 5 mins
1 cup mixed fruit
1 cup water
2 oz butter

Add

1 cup SR flour
1 cup sugar
1 tsp baking soda

Steam 2 hours
Apply custard

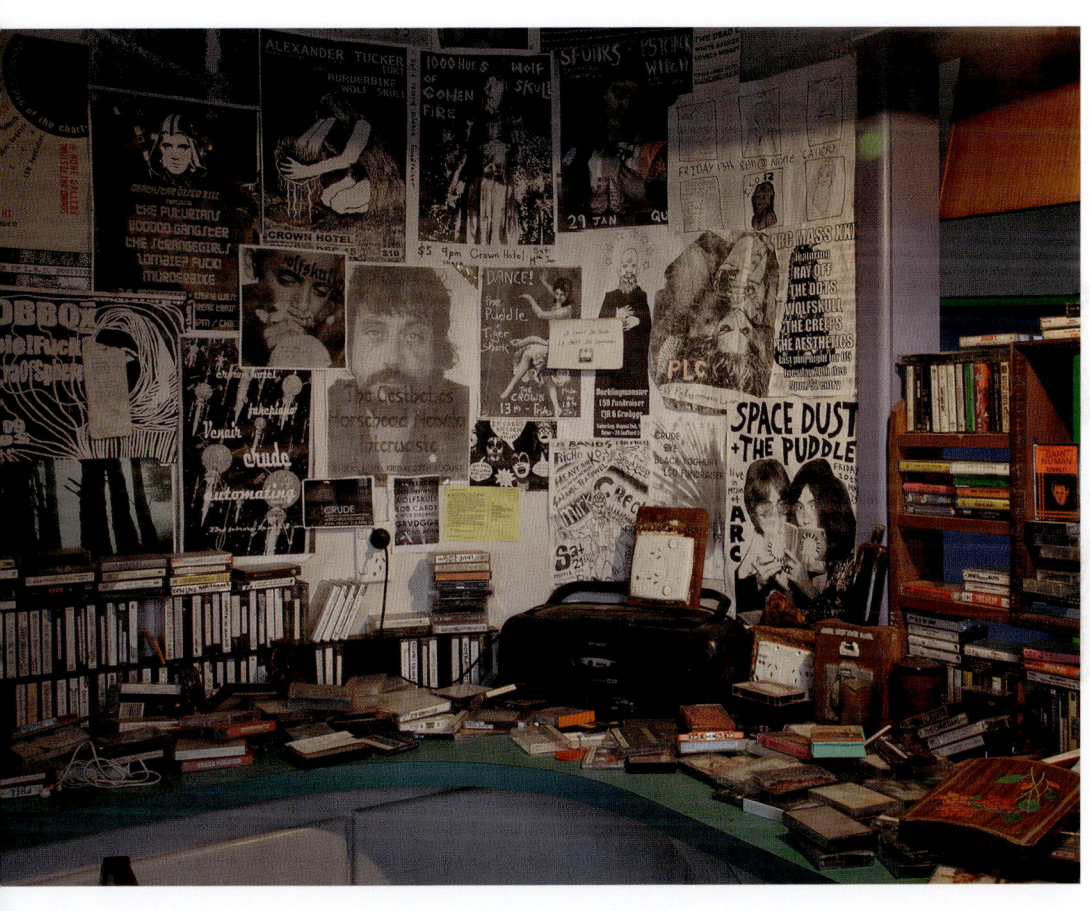

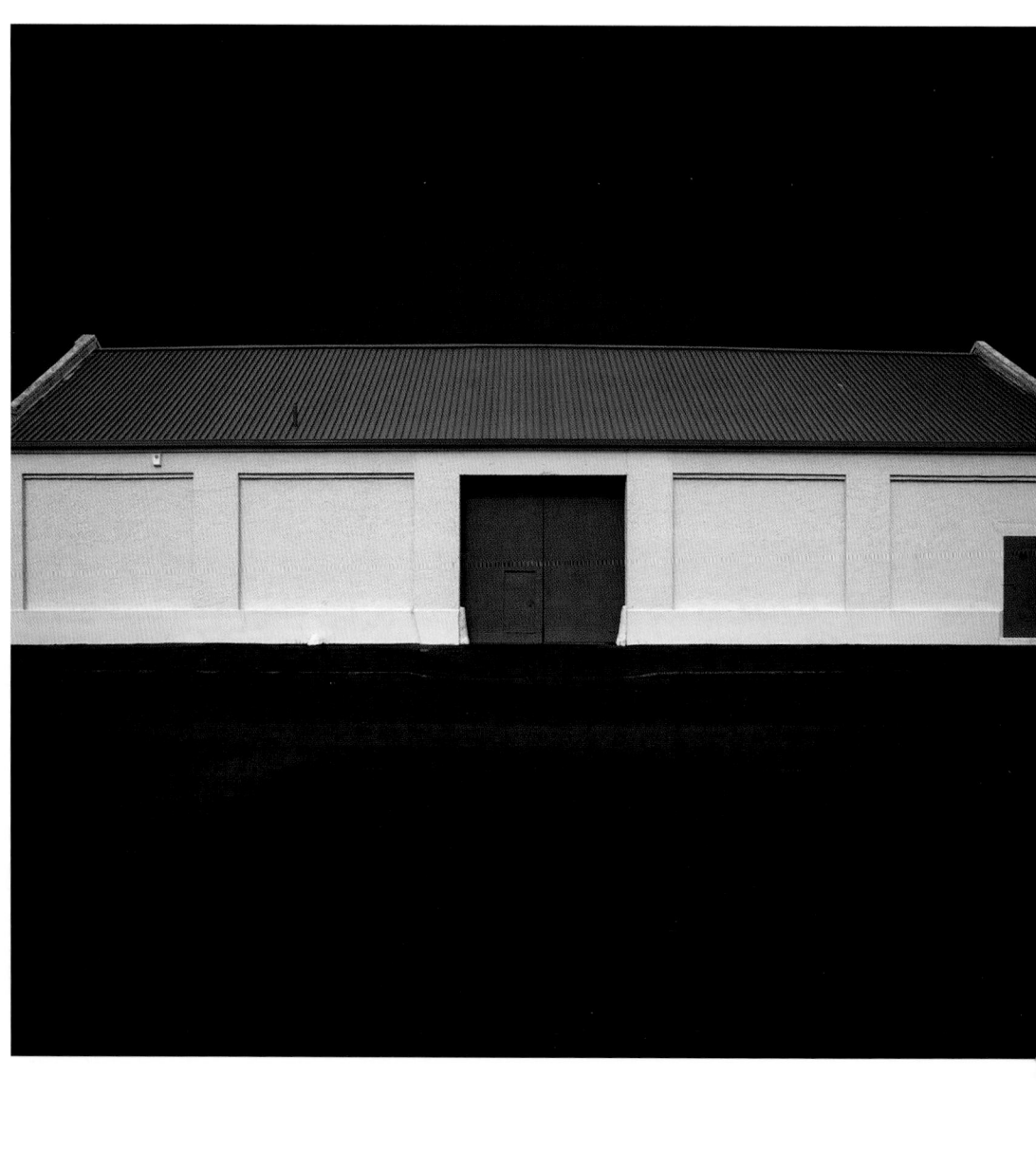

HEIDI NORTH

Babes in the Woods

The crawfish stew travelled hundreds of miles with him, from Louisiana to Savannah, on the cracked black leather back seat of his rental car. Later, she would throw it up in the toilet of the cheap hotel room when he left again.

He had hit a deer on his way to her. Damaged the rental. The sleek navy side of the car buckled inwards. It alarmed her to see how something seeming so solid could just crumple up like shimmery crepe paper, the kind you wrapped flowers in. She couldn't picture the road he had taken; this part of the country baffled her. She had been here four months, driving across state lines. She would have asked more questions; she liked to get a picture of things. She was hungry for him, wanting to know everything—where he had been without her, what he saw—but she was distracted by the kid clambering out from the back seat.

It was the first time she had met the daughter. The girl was six, maybe seven. Hard to tell how old exactly when the kid stood by the car with her skinny legs in her pink shorts. Popping gum. She was button cute. Huge smile. Each one of her many black braids finished with a hot pink elastic.

'Surprise!' Jimmy threw her an easy grin.

And it was, at first, and then not. He had already talked about getting married.

The kid held out the stew to her in an old-fashioned clay pot, covered in clingfilm. The press of red strained against the thin plastic—presumably from the impact of the crash—but she had to hand it to the covering: it had held firm. The kid passed over the whole thing without a trace of shyness, just a huge smile. She wondered what Jimmy had told the kid about her. This strange blonde woman with a funny voice.

She carried the stew inside the hotel room. It was heavier than it had looked in that six-year-old's arms. She put in on the counter and peeled off the it clingfilm, lifting off several congealed lumps of tomato and craw in the process, listening to the kid chatter. The kid's name was Suzie. She liked ponies and pink. She was eight.

73

The stew, cold like this, confused her. She pushed aside the remains of yesterday's takeaways—limp, cold chips she knew she would never eat—to put the pot in the fridge and threw the whole congealed mess of the plasticy covering into the sink.

She was waiting for him to touch her. And when he did, coming up behind her at the sink, running his warm hands under her flimsy cotton singlet around onto her smooth stomach, skin to skin, sliding the hard callouses on his palms onto her hip bones, slipping down, she felt the looseness, the raw need.

They put the TV on for the kid while they got busy in the bathroom. There wasn't much of a selection of DVDs, and he hadn't thought ahead. The kid seemed happy enough though, with her makeshift babysitter, sitting cross-legged in the centre of the unmade double bed, eating a packet of crisps, watching Ricki Lake.

He pushed her against the bathroom door, put his hand over her mouth and whispered in her ear, 'You gonna take care of Daddy?' His accent rolled through her like a wave, heading for the break. He held one hand around her throat as she came. The thrill was unbearable.

When they were done, she peeled her panties off the floor. They were damp with the spill from the shower but she put them back on anyway. Pulled down her skirt, smoothing the crumples out of the cornflower pattern, snapped up her bra. She bent slightly to fix her hair in the small wall mirror, black age spots blooming in the corners. He stood behind her. Still naked. Still hard.

'You're unbelievable.' He ran his dark hands down her pale arms.

'Yeah?' She smiled at him through the warp of the mirror. She had that look she got after sex. Her hair was all mussed up, the makeup ruined. The lines of her forehead were pronounced.

'You're the best I've ever had.' He nudged into her.

She wanted to ask him what his plan was, but she couldn't find the words. She wanted him to stay with her, in this cheap roadside hotel she had ended up in. Maybe the three of them could stay there a while. Maybe forever.

His hands were travelling under her skirt again. She smiled, shifting away from him slightly. The kid was right through the door. She noticed her mascara had run, black clouds under her eyes. She started unsmudging them, scraping the black off with her broken fingernail.

'I love you.' His fingers were knots in her hair. This wasn't the first time he had said this to her.

They'd met two weeks earlier in a club in Raceland, near New Orleans. She'd had two bourbons already, so was brave enough to approach him. His skin was the colour of burnt coffee. She had an overwhelming desire to stroke right where his t-shirt met his arms. He had been visiting his brother in hospital and needed a drink afterwards. It was 3pm on a Tuesday.

She asked, joking, to see his ID.

He twisted to reveal his six-pack abs, a line of dark hair running down his belly button, as he located his wallet in his tight blue jeans. He handed his driver's licence over to her, bemused at her behaviour, her accent, the strange flatness of her vowels.

She introduced him to the couple she was travelling with, Zara and Ari. She took him back to the hotel room they were all sharing. They watched his home videos of a hurricane and then a wedding, all four of them lying on the bed. She shifted so her skirt rode high, her leg pressed next to his. He couldn't get enough of their foreignness.

'And what about Māori people?' he asked, 'Do you know any?'

He had so many questions. 'Do you all live together or do you live in separate parts of the country?'

She didn't know what to tell him. Zara started laughing and Ari brought up the Treaty of Waitangi. She didn't know how to explain, so they got their own hotel room and screwed on a brown polyester duvet studded with other people's cigarette burns.

They went for breakfast at Denny's. He said he'd never seen a white girl eat so much before. They had another beer and played some pool. She smoked but he didn't really mind.

When he left her late that afternoon she thought that might be the end of it. But he came back the next night after dark with a picnic of soul food—fettuccini, turkey necks, beef bristle, catfish—and they ate it by the flatness of the Savannah River.

He drove her around, showing her the sights. Lil Wayne the only CD in the five-track CD player. He put his hand on her thigh. She noticed with delight the bulge in his jeans.

They wound up that night at a hotel in a bad area of New Orleans. She didn't know where they were, only that Jimmy sauntered in a way she had only ever seen before in movies. He gave her the car keys, warm metal hitting her open palm, with an easy grin. 'We're gonna be fine. No one's gonna believe you're not a cop—a white girl like you in this neighbourhood.'

He unbuttoned her shirt before he had even shut the door. She didn't see the bullet hole in it until they were done. By then he had already asked her to marry him in a way that didn't imply a question. Just a fact. 'When we're married, baby cake, I'm gonna love you all the way to California.'

Somewhere between the bourbon and cokes and the sex she told him she was heading to Georgia with Zara and Ari. There had been a reason, somewhere along the line, but she had forgotten it. Maybe it was because Zara's nan had been from there. Or maybe it was something else. She couldn't remember any more. The three of them had been on the road too long—four months, maybe more. All she had known was she was leaving that place. She had forgotten the taste of the air back home.

When they met Jimmy they were supposed to be looking for work. But Zara and Ari seemed to have enough cash for the three of them to get by. They had done scraps here and there, most recently dishwashing at a backpackers in Raceland. But the car had been itching to drive and they had given in. When she left Raceland, Jimmy had given her a lifting smile, slid his hand into her panties and hooked a finger deep inside her. Zara and Ari looked away.

'I'll come for you,' he said.

And he had. Crawfish stew and kid in tow.

He dressed now in the early afternoon light, kissed her and exited the bathroom.

'I'm gonna take you to Tybee Island, baby girl,' he told the kid, switching off the TV.

Despite having been both a US Marine and a coke dealer in a past life, he seemed terrified of the water, and she had to urge him to swim. She took his hand, and the kid's hand, and all joined together the three of them waded out to a little sand island. The light was golden. Everything shimmered. The sun hit their faces in a way that hid their eyes. An old guy with only one leg asked her if Jimmy was her husband.

'Not yet,' Jimmy said, winking.

She blushed. But she could see the edges of it, a life out here in the sun.

Suzie looked up at her. 'You gonna swim with me?' Her face was flush with light.

'Sure, baby girl,' she replied. His language sounded funny in her mouth.

On the way back to the hotel they got stuck in traffic. Ahead of them a bridal party—the bride a smash of tulle anxious to get to her wedding. It seemed like a sign.

The light was flattening. She had drunk too much beer. They had to stop for her to piss on the side of the road. Some redneck slowed down and yelled out the window, 'You gonna get bit by snakes.'

Back at the hotel they found Zara and Ari had come back. They drank bourbon and cokes and ate the crawfish stew under the hot stars. It was unlike anything she had ever eaten before.

A long time after dark Jimmy put the kid to bed in the car. The twisted metal of the bonnet was a refusal of beauty in the darkness. It gave her a pang, seeing Suzie fall asleep on the cracked leather back seat, legs twined around a patchwork blanket. She was too old for teddy bears, but Suzie clutched a pale grey one tucked up tight under her chin.

'You sure she'll be all right?' she asked Jimmy, running her fingers over the impossible softness of the sleeping child's cheek. She imagined putting her to sleep in a real bed in a real house, crisp white sheets lifting in the summer breeze. There was a bud of feeling in her like hope.

Jimmy laughed and led her back into the hotel room, spreading her legs on the bed that still held the imprint of the kid's body.

She woke up at 4am, raw and startled. Reaching for a water bottle that wasn't there, she realised he wasn't there any more either. She pulled herself to the window. Her head pounding. The car was gone.

The water bottle lay empty on the floor. She reached for the dregs of bourbon instead, not turning on the light. Just sitting naked in the sweaty darkness, drinking.

Later, barely making it to the bathroom, the stew splattered against the cracking yellow tiles. Even throwing it up, retching, knees bruising with the imprints of the cold tile floor, it was still the best thing she had ever tasted.

Hours might have passed. She pulled herself up from the bathroom floor, felt her way cat-like through the night down towards the vending machine outside the reception. She was parched. She already knew she would never see Jimmy again.

There was a stranger down there, outside the row of empty motel units. A pale stretched-out version of a boy. She should have been afraid—it was still dark, she was underdressed, drunk—but she was reckless with sadness.

The boy watched her as she fumbled coins into the vending machine. The money still unfamiliar in her hands.

'Nice morning,' he said.

'Is it?' She looked towards him, squinting against the white halo of strip lights around his head. He was just a baby. All of them, just babes in the woods.

'Whereabouts you from?' the boy asked, clocking her accent.

She put the can, wet with dew, close to her cheek to feel the cool, thought of how she had touched the kid's hot cheek just hours ago. She closed her eyes. The darkness there was a sort of remedy. It was only while answering she realised what she was saying was true. 'I don't know.'

JOY HOLLEY

Ode to Pomegranate

Tomorrow, you will have lived 19 years.
You still won't have seen one in the flesh,
nor the skin—
thick and red.

You have seen plenty of girls
in the flesh,
many of them beautiful
in it.

No exception: she
is from a place
where pomegranates grow
in a friend's back yard.

She has eaten
with her fingers
in an unmade bed.
She has stained the sheets

sweet. You wonder,
should you give her the little white card?
Stolen from the letter set?
The bargain bin? The bookshop?

Inside you'll write
a poem; a prayer
to Persephone,
in hope that

perhaps, she'll melt
the squares of snow
your mother pinned to the wall
last January.

A premature pick
of the crop. Placenta-like
in your hand as
popped pips fall past

your thumb: the only pills
she can prescribe.
But you keep on trawling fruit shops,
finding only persimmons.

JOHN PRINS

A Good Man

It is important to Adam that he drives me to the gym, so there I am, on his doorstep in my shorts and sneakers. I knock and Adam, shirtless, possibly naked, swoops behind the door as it swings away. He calls that he'll be out in five, just has to take a shit.

Six minutes later, we are on the road.

'You told Jake?' says Adam.

'No,' I say.

'No?'

'Not yet.'

'Good shit, you're a good mate.'

'I don't know.'

'No, you're good. You're, you're, what's that word, chivalrous.'

'That's not what chivalry means.'

'Sure it is, we both are, both noble as fuck.'

'I think chivalry is you holding the door for Eve, not, well, not what you're doing.'

'Slamming her door,' he punches my arm and I swear.

'It's not like he loved her.'

'Loved her?' says Adam. 'The fuck.' He looks at me as though I am a stranger.

'He'll be fine.'

'Say it started last weekend.'

'When *did* it start?'

'Last weekend.'

I laugh.

'Easter weekend,' he says.

'Since Easter!'

'Well, it's done now, can't be undone, can it? I can't un-fuck her.'

Then we are in the gym. Air is being pumped in and out, it carries the smell of disinfected sweat and sweet peat. Large men live inside the walls, concerned only with the image of themselves. Adam, wearing a singlet, is flat on his back on a bench, which disappears beneath his bulk so that it looks like he is defying gravity. I stand at his head, spotting he calls it, I call it keeping a promise.

'Two, phoow, three, phoow, four, phoow, Phoove, Phraugh.' Adam slams the bar back on its stand.

'Wow, nice,' I say.

I suggest lending him the novel I am reading after I finish because I think he'll like it.

'Keep it,' he says.

'It's good, it's about this kid learning how devious people can be.'

'Don't have time to read.'

'It's good.'

'The thing about books,' he says, 'is that no book is ever about me.'

'Have you read any …'

'I haven't read shit, it's always these wordy chicks who think about shit all the time or by some skinny dude with all sorts of feelings and shit, and it's always about a fucken writer.'

The bench is damp when I lie down and the sponge has been worn away so that my teeth want to grind against the texture of it. 'Can you take off those two big ones on the ends?' I say.

'Who the fuck wants to read about a writer?'

'You're right.'

'Fucken writers.'

'Always writing about writers.'

'Or their parents.'

'About skinny dudes with daddy issues.'

'Daddy issues. See, my dad's a fucken legend. Where is that story? The one about how much a kid loves his dad.'

'So, you'd be into it if you found a book about you.' I push the bar up off its cradle and put it back down again. 'No, too much, take off one more.'

'Could be. Right, go. Arms after this. Go!'

'Three, phoow, four, phau, five, phew, Pharrgh.'

'Come on, come on, go go gih. Good man. Right, arms time. Didn't talk much but man, a real hero.'

'How long ago did he—?'

'Couple of years. Nah man, fucken legend. Proper hero. Built his business from nothing. On the tools for a couple of years then owned that shit.'

Adam makes us do the backs of our arms, our chests again and then some ab stuff. My body, not used to this sort of abuse, feels fit to burst. Adam's gait changes during the session, as though he is being tightened up from the inside, ratcheted up, coiled, cranking and clicking.

Back in his truck, Adam moves quickly through the gears. Holding the handle above my head, I observe my outline and muscle forms on the corners and I feel shame at my narcissism.

'Look at those guns!' he says, following my gaze. 'Yew! Curls get the girls, man.'

'I'm pretty sure that is curly hair. Curly hair gets the girls. Curls.'

'Shit no, guns get the girls and look at those things! Come on shithead, move!' He gives the horn a burst. 'Girls are gonna love you.'

'I'm okay.'

'Girls are gonna look at those guns and think about fucking. Straight away.' Adam leans over and punches my arm. 'Bang, fucken bang,' he says. It hurts and I flinch.

'Hey!' He looks at me.

'What?' I'm acutely aware of the road in front of us.

'That story about my dad. I remember when I was young, about five, and we got this pig. We were given it by an uncle, or it was Dad's payment for a job he had done, I don't know, whatever. He was always fucken working, man, and he gets this pig. It's small, he can carry it in his arms like a baby, and we keep it in the dog kennel. I don't ever remember playing with it, I mean shit, a pig living in your back yard? I would have definitely wanted to play with that pig but I don't ever remember doing it.

'So summer comes and Christmas and it's hot and I'm probably climbing a tree. *Indicate, dickhead!* We had this big tree out back and Dad comes out and sends me inside and says something like "Stay inside." He's all serious and shit. I know something is up so of course the only place I want to be is outside, doing whatever my dad is doing, right? It's what you do, right? I used to whittle sticks with this old Swiss army knife just to be doing something with a knife, just like Dad was always doing something with a knife—

plucking a duck or gutting a deer. He'd fucken walk for hours and carry a carcass like a backpack, blood pouring down his neck and shoulders, you know, where he's cut the head off. Weighs a tonne, the head.

'I remember there were always photos in the house of Dad hunting—standing behind dead animals, or holding them up. Holding the head towards the camera as though they were a couple of old buddies who'd been asked to smile. One of these photos I remember had Dad and a deer turned into a backpack walking through some smoke or smudge or thick grass or something and I remember feeling so bad for him having to walk through that shitty dark forest. Then a few years later, looking at the photo again, I figured out what the smudge was and how fucken stupid I had been. The smudge wasn't a forest, it was the finger of the person who took the photo, their finger covering the lens.

'Shit I wanted to be like him though, so much. Once while I was in the garage and a mate of Dad's was around—I can't have been more than five or six—and I said, real casual, 'Right, I'm taking a piss.' And they looked at me and I can't remember what they said but man, they had a laugh. Dad even shot a deer once with a baby deer inside her and they cut it out and it was alive. It lived for a couple of days at our house, then it died and Dad had it stuffed and kept it on his bedside table.

'So anyway, Dad's definitely up to something in the back yard and I know it and I want in on it. He's locked me inside the house so I climb up onto the washing machine— must have dragged a chair over or something. I could climb when I was little, man—spent half my life in that big old tree out the back. So I'm peeking out the window, the curtains are blowing in my face. It's so vivid. Crazy how some shit just gets stuck in there.' He's pointing at his head. 'Bloody branded in there.

'And I'm peeking out and Dad goes to the kennel. He's got a massive fucken knife in one hand and the pig's food bowl in the other. Eggshells, lettuce, potato skins, that sort of shit, and he opens the kennel and puts the bowl of food down in the middle of the grass. I'm confused by the food. I know what the knife means but the food, the food is fucking with me.

'The pig is not leaving that kennel. It knows, man. They say they know and I believe them. It knew all right. It took one look at the big steel blade and at Dad's eyes and it wasn't leaving that kennel for shit.

'So Dad puts the knife down, puts it around the corner, out of the pig's sight. The pig is not buying that shit, though. Dad has to climb into the kennel on his hands and knees and pulls it out by its collar.

'Yeah, it had a collar, but no name. It's weird. The pig squeals and struggles and dad is so fucken calm and I can't watch any more. I look at the wallpaper. Then the pig stops squealing. I look again, real slow. The pig has its head down and it is chewing on some lettuce. Dad is kneeling down beside it and he's talking to it. I can't hear him but he is definitely saying something and he's patting the pig on its back and he gives the pig's ears a ruffle. You know, like you would to a dog, and I loved my dad for scratching that pig's ears the way he did. The pig is real calm now and it's hooking into the food like it's the most normal thing that ever happened. It's a nice fucken moment, you know?

'I don't see where Dad goes because I'm watching the pig, watching it munching its food and I've got this dumb grin on. Then something catches my eye and I swear Dad looked straight at me, he definitely looked at me, this big knife swinging in his hand and he looks straight at me, looks at the pig, kneels back down to where he was, ruffles those big floppy ears, steps over its back and runs the knife under its neck. Blood splashes all over the lettuce and I jump off that washing machine as quick as I can and run into my room and shut the door and jump under the covers and cry like a fucken five-year-old.

'That pig never squealed at the end though—stayed silent, kept its dignity, man. *Move, go go, ah shit! Orange means go, you dumb shit!* We never talked about it. Mum and Dad shared these shitty jokes about how good the ham tasted that year and I knew, man. I fucken knew and they knew and nobody said a word. I still can't decide if I wish I'd never seen it, still don't know if a kid can know too much about something like that. Still don't know if Dad knew I was watching—never asked him.

'So when you seeing Jake again?' he says.

'When I see him,' I say.

'And you'll tell him.'

'I'll tell him,' I say.

Adam massages the defined parts of himself and tells me I'm a good man.

'You think that pig had a good life?' I say.

'Shit man, what even is a good life for a pig?'

'You think the pig was in pain?'

'Not at the end but before, in the bit before Dad dragged him out, in that bit there, where there was panic in him, if that's what pain is then fuck yeah, he was in pain. When you tell Jake, though, make sure I'm not the bad guy.'

'Not the bad guy, got it.'

'You're a good man,' says Adam, and he punches me in the arm for the third time that day and it hurts like fuck.

TUSIATA AVIA

Tualima/Hand tattoo

My father with a hand on my hand as I row the *Lady Tusiata*
a correction—pull this way—and he lays the net
and I row him into the middle of the Waimakariri
cold water, fast currents—he reaches out to guide my hand
I hold him in the river—I am 10, maybe 11—I hold him in the sweeping
and he lays the upega, calls the fa`alupega from the va
we will catch what is swimming there.

I sit at the formica table—we have moved it over the dividing line
between here and over there. We are here now
right over the kneeling place, the hittingcrying place
under us is the new mat, green diamonds like malu
the ones you buy in Otara and bring back here.

Tyla sits opposite me. Around me sit the women I can see—
see Danielle (the ones I can't will use her eyes and hands and they will get heavy).
See Serah. See Tanya. See Louise. See Ana. See the one, they are not a woman,
see Khye. I watch them all, they are my upega.
We have already spread the upega of seawater and smoke
and the birds and sun in the front yard have done their own clearing out
every room grows its own flowers: white for Louise, red for Serah and Sala
yellow for Tanya, purple for Khye, green for Danielle.

We sit in this house, it is clean now—all these women and the one who is not
have walked it for me. I don't need to cast anything
no hidings on the lounge room floor—I don't need to chase anything
these women net the house for me.
The one who caused me pain is now my kaitiaki
he puts his hands on my head and they wipe away my tears.

Tyla draws the malu for protection, for upega, for fish and birds
that trek across the worlds and fly between them. Dad draws in close
hand on my hand on the oar, he lays the net, he lays the net
the fa`alupega floats out behind us, before us
Danielle's hands are getting heavy now.

Tyla lays the net into my skin, cut by cut, I watch my father bait the hook
I watch him cast the rod into the river, then hold the wriggling fish still
in his big hand and with the other, pull the hook glinting for a moment
in the reflected sun, from the tender bloodied mouth.

Such concentration on the tautai's face as she lays the upega one cut, one cut
I look up for a moment, there is a woman standing over her—older, darker—
hand on her hand. This house is heaving with tupuaga today.
One cut, one cut, one hook, one hook, one breath, one breath
I hold the dinghy in the currents of the Waimakariri as Tyla lays the net.

And at the end Ana signals I should dance like a taupou
even though I am 51 now and when I bow my knees crack
loud as the popping of fish eyes.
Before Tanya cries, before my mother kisses me, before my daughter
and all the women and the one who isn't the women aiuli me in the siva
before I lift the photo of Dad—the young black and white Mikaio—
before he was a va`a in the River through Pulotu
before I lift him to my forehead

the tupuaga come across the window and I can see them this time
the woman with the fuzzy hair the one as dark as the Solomons,
the one with the bowl of oil
I don't need to ask Danielle what this means because even I know
this is meant for healing.

Notes appear on page 178

CIARAN FOX

South (from N.E.W.S. from the twenty-ninth floor)

Montreal

I have a paper cup and some dirty socks
and the city lets me have this bench
sometimes. It's a privilege.
Sleeping fourteen hours
or so, there ain't much to do
and I'm free of your judgement.
From on high, a heart blocks out the sun
I'm as invisible as pain to progress.
Hope is thin as newspaper blankets,
as poetry from the twenty-ninth floor.
Down here, it's raining eggshells.

VICTOR BILLOT

Facebook Sends a Memory

Facebook sends a memory
of the then preceding now:
child and mother sunk
under summer's glow.
Things were good
and things were bad.
Pixels map deceits
that hold sweet truth.
This tactless friend
exhumes dead time
from layered ash.
Now the child has grown
into the future's gaoh.
As midnight creeps,
tap, swipe and pinch.

BRYAN WALPERT

Experiments Touching Cold (1)

after Robert Boyle

If you needed any evidence
that even so extremely close
a medium as glass,
as Boyle eloquently put it,
is not able to hinder
the transmission of cold,
it is here centuries later
in this second-storey window
through which you look
today onto the garden
where even in such intemperate
conditions she works her shears
and pulls up weeds,
less—it would seem by the evidence
of such weather as there is today—
to ensure the efficacy of the task
than to gather to herself
the necessary space unavailable
because not wholly physical
in a house otherwise occupied,
and though it is tempting
to rap upon the window, its attempt
would simply leave her in the difficult
position of deciding whether
to acknowledge the fact of the sound,
and in craning her neck toward it
the fact that she is not alone,

so it is best to leave her there,
to step away from the pane,
recalling, to return to Boyle,
that in vessels not hermetically
sealed it may be pretended
that the coldness of the internal air
is merely communicated by some
unheeded but immediate
intercourse with the external.

SIOBHAN HARVEY

Someone Other than Yourself

They are but dressings of a former sight
—Shakespeare, Sonnet CXXIII

And now autumn draws close, the ghost of
the woman and country you once were resurfaces
like the seasons, to haunt the lives and landscapes
you've left behind; such memories, such grief.

This is what happens to those who migrate. Time
continues unchanged as someone other than yourself
takes their first breath, watches your plane inhale
the sky, returns to your apartment, their footsteps
upon its wooden floor echoing in your heart. Mirror;

writing desk; writing paper; the bed you slept late in:
these furnish their soul as well as your own. As you
arrive on foreign soil, they write an elegy. As you
wed, they compose a sonnet. As your son is born,
their collection delivers them the Forward Prize.

Yet this is what you miss most: your anorexia and abuse
revived by someone other than yourself; your estranged
parents reconciled to someone also other than yourself. Nothing
novel; nothing strange. Tomorrow you'll return to the place
—an old street, an old house—you left. Ajar, an old door

will disclose an old mirror holding a reflection of someone
other than yourself as footsteps, echoes in the heart, draw close.

MADELEINE CHILD

The Sheepshed of Earthly Delights

It would be our big sister who spotted the hand-painted sign, 'Eden Hore's World of Fashion', banged onto a fencepost out in the back of beyond; who made us turn down a gravelly road, past parched paddocks of dusty daggy sheep to a great blot of a corrugated iron shed by a brick farmhouse. We bleated. Eden wasn't around, but some woman gave us a tour of the collection—opening up half a kilometre of purpose-built wardrobes and pulling out racks of flouncy gowns and gushing over a particularly something teal-dyed hand-spun Romney hogget fleece thing with peacock feathers attached.

We heard about the early Scottish settlers; about the Hores farming here for generations and Glenshee being the Hore family homestead—'from the garlic Glen Sith, meaning Glen of the Fairies'; about Eden not being much into it, instead converting the shearing shed and 'diversifying', at first into sheepy garments of wool and suede but then these high-fashion gowns à la Miss World.

We giggled. We sniggered. My sister snorted that we were all so *parochial*, and flounced ahead. We straggled along behind, dully, but when we heard about Eden's vision to turn the farm into a safari park my little sister was off, imagining giraffes and echidnas and rounding me up into a fantasy about a tiger cub that escapes and we find it up by Clunie's sod cottage and sneak it food, and it like only trusts *us* and is our secret and tame but still wild and then and then and like and then.

But I had my own flight of fancy going on—ever since a neighbour had dropped by that morning to warn us that a youth from the Waipiata naughty boys' home up the road was on the loose.

ESSA MAY RANAPIRI

echidna: born of eve and lucifer

they meet underneath the apples on the sabbath to fuck in the bushes
she couldn't help but love it when the forked tongue made an electric feast
of her soft flesh   such a division she never felt while being another man's
rib   she knows all the scales in the world   and knows the snake is
a liar   but why shouldn't she be able to have some fun   while it lasts
and adam is as thick as a post anyway   always finishing too fast
with adam   she was a way   for the first man to jack himself off
the serpent   cared about her   pleasure   at least

ESSA MAY RANAPIRI

echidna: half woman half snake

she lies in the desert her twin tails stretched out   split out underneath her
she travels miles and miles and miles   living off the dust of the land
thanking her great grandmother for   the food
oh Papatūānuku how good are thou   how good
she makes it to the coast   the sun plays with the chop of the wave
she takes to the water to pledge   allegiance to her great-grandfather Tangaroa
a daughter of Tū-te-wehiwehi   he had to have a Pākehā name didn't he?
Sat on   what did he sit on?   she admits she could have misheard
as she floats nymphal in the
ocean

MICHAEL HALL

1970 Something

I played Moses once
In a small Waikato town children's play—
Or so the story goes.
According to Mum and Dad
I was unrecognisable
Normally I didn't have much to say.
Your son was magnificent, people said.
Where did that come from?
He's such a natural.

I have no memory of it.
I do not know if I parted the sea.
Or brought prophetic words
Down off Mt Te Aroha, thundering
About everyone's heads.
Or led my people
Across the stage.

After that, I returned
To being a child, grew up, remembered
Other things. Some days
I can feel the desert shadows
Play across my face. And sometimes
Something I would like to proclaim
Almost seizes me—
Though I'm not sure what it is.
It was just a children's stage.
But for a moment

There I was: tinily robed and ablaze.

JODIE DALGLEISH

Love Letter

I'll cut out
the word 'love' first

make a cento
of such delicate
paper, touch

of my wrist my fingers
turning and resting on

glances of skin's text to the split
slightness of each page, cleft

into enactments, fragments
as sheer as white corpuscular tissue.

A veining of us together,
at the end
of my finepaper knife
and stuck down tight, forever.

FRANKIE McMILLAN

The Bride from Clarry's Vineyard

So we're just finishing up the wedding cakes when I remember we haven't placed the little bride and bridegroom on the top of the one for Clarry's Vineyard and I look at the order just to check it's not two of the same; two brides in white or two grooms in black which is becoming more common these days, and Johnny wipes his hands on his apron and says we've got to get more ventilation in here, the iced flowers aren't looking too perky, and I point to the order and say who took this order and Johnny says what's wrong with it and I say there's something missing, that's what wrong and Johnny shuffles forward, back hunched as a hamster and stares at the paper for so long, pity takes hold and I say, look here there's only one figurine put down for the top tier of the cake … *so who's she going to marry, huh?* And we hold the order up to the light from the window but there's nothing ticked there and Johnny says maybe there's not supposed to be another figure and now my kindness towards Johnny, working in the bakery for twenty-five years, my kindness starts to harden like a ball of sugar at 340°F and I bark at him, how can that be, what are you trying to say, and I push past him to the decoration drawers and pull out a handful of plastic brides and bridegrooms and I say, *sort it, Johnny.*

But even as I'm banging the drawers shut and even as he bends down to wipe the sweat off his forehead I know, just as I know about climate warming, and infertility, and too much plastic in the ocean, and the rising divorce rate, I know there's a bride out there without a bridegroom and she'll walk alone through Clarry's vineyard and before the priest she'll put her own ring on her own finger and this is just the beginning of other brides all over the country walking alone on their wedding day and what I'm going to do with all the extra plastic bridegrooms in the drawer, I don't know.

ELIZABETH KIRKBY-MCLEOD

A Matter of Timing

A doctor tells the father about his life;
its giving, getting, keeping.

A doctor tells him about his mind;
its forming, finishing, falling.

When his time is over, the father
climbs to the top of the Woolworths

building, wanting to find a door
opening out to the sky.

And when he doesn't, when
he finds the clock is still counting

correct time, with perfect pacing,
he sits and sticks the seconds

together, holding the hands, wondering
how to stop it from winning.

TREVOR HAYES

Aerodynamics

A man on a park bench has a paper bag
of letters he feeds to small books that flutter
around him and flap their pages. They're hungry
for the letters to make the words that write
their contents. There are many unfinished texts
and the books feed to become themselves.

One is on the verge of becoming a read that 'instructs
and entertains in equal measures'. Another needs the words
to keep bombs from falling over the city, so beautifully
portrayed as the backdrop to their eccentric love story.
Some require only referencing and/or an index.

One book on the fringes
is too thin, barely
gets the crumbs it needs
to fall down pages
into poems
investigating the inadequacies
of language
and how that's what
it'll fly with.

THOM CONROY

The Jacket

On the flight to Invercargill our plane travelled through a cloudscape of silver-limned mesas and entered a cavern of cloud, our wingtips going pink in the vaulted, floorless chambers, one engulfing another, while a shimmering abyss opened beneath. As if borne aloft by the grandeur, we punctured the caliginous dome and surfaced on broad and golden steppes, the vertical faces of which were pocked with a fretwork of grottos, great unfurling porticos and backlit loggia. As we ascended the final steppe, cloud curled like the closing sides of a parted sea through which we had been granted passage, and in the moment before the two walls united, a runnel of honeyed sunlight rushed into the gap, blanking out the windows in a haze of illumination.

In the next moment the cloud closed and all went grey. I sat there speechless, dumbstruck. A spell had been cast, its brilliance raining through my vision as I turned to take in the reactions of other passengers. But I saw that not a single other person had noticed. A woman sat across the aisle swiping her tablet. A crying baby was being hushed.

The flight attended paused beside me. *Did I have any rubbish?*

My business in Invercargill was unremarkable. I volunteered as a deputy on a disputes tribunal and had been asked to fill in for a hearing involving an inheritance. I would be staying overnight, attending the hearing in the morning, and making a long flight home in the afternoon.

Once I had checked into my motel, I walked along a wide street of big box stores and petrol stations. I found a non-descript café, and, against my strict habit, overate. To walk it off, I decided to wander through the bitter cold of twilight.

I made my way through a residential neighbourhood, peering at rusted swing sets and elaborate black growths of mould on the white walls, dimly aware that I would never tread this street again. Curtains were drawn and browning cabbage trees rattled in the wind. In the passing cars, the people did not glance at me.

Eventually I saw someone cycling toward me in a red flannel jacket. It was a man, much younger than me, unhelmeted. He might not have caught my eye except that, even at a distance, I recognised something—or thought I recognised something—about this man. Was it his posture? His dark head of long, thick hair? As he came nearer I saw that there was a certain intensity in his look, and, as I noticed this, I understood that this was what I found familiar. At one time I had had this very same look. I had also travelled everywhere on a bike, always without a helmet. I had never, however, worn a red flannel jacket.

The man rode directly toward me, coming very close before he turned sharply into the driveway of a dismal-looking home. Not wishing to stare, I turned away. But the moment I broke the man's gaze, a quiver took hold of me—a terrible, strange trembling as if I were experiencing a fever, for I knew then that this man was me. He was twenty-five years younger, yes, and he was a person distinct from me, but at the same time I knew for a fact that this man was undeniably me.

I turned and walked back to the house in time to see the front door closing. There was no question of what to do next. I rushed to the door, determined to knock, but I found I could not bring myself to do it, and so I made my way back to the motel. I undressed, brushed my teeth. As I was looking in the mirror I saw my face, and it startled me. Unconsciously, I had been thinking of myself with the face I saw on this younger man: a leaner, tighter face of jet-black stubble.

Though I felt a powerful desire to avoid interfering in this stranger's life, I understood that I had to do something. I dressed again, made my way back through the desolate streets of homes with their small, bare patches of grass. There was an unfamiliar smell in the air, and though I had never experienced it first hand, I knew it meant it was going to snow.

As I came upon the house where I had seen this other, younger me, the first flakes were floating to earth, cold points of white that stung my skin as I crept along the driveway into the back garden. There was an intermittent whoosh of traffic and a trickle of wind in the air, and I suppose it was this white noise that muffled my approach, for as I rounded the back of the house I saw the glow of a cigarette in the dark.

But what I had witnessed was the final, desperate draw of nicotine, and the very moment it registered, the point of pink light went sailing off into the dark where it was flicked. A figure turned without the least glance in my direction. The back door slammed closed. I was alone.

I crept to the window beside the door. There was no curtain, and inside it was dark, except for the light of a TV illuminated by two animated race cars and the words 'New Game'. I saw someone pass in front of the screen. I heard two voices, both male. I stepped aside and flattened myself against the wall while bits of snow stuck to my glasses.

I had to leave of course. I had to get away from there and never return. There was no question. None at all. On the other hand, I found I could not move. I listened, but there were no more voices. After a few minutes I felt the wall behind my back shaking as someone walked the length of the house. A door closed.

When I peered inside again the TV was off. At first I thought it was too dark to see anything inside, but as I stood there I realised that the streetlight through the front windows lit up the room sufficiently that I could make out the dim outlines of furniture. My eyes adjusted and I took in the layout of the room and, in time, the shape of a figure lying on the couch. By the time I heard the soft grinding of a snore I was shivering so badly I found it difficult to move.

The door stuck, but it was unlocked, and came open with the sound of wood against wood. I waited, one hand on the knob. The snoring had ceased and I felt that I was about to be caught breaking and entering some stranger's home. Only I wasn't breaking, was I? And he was not a stranger. I pushed the door shut without latching it, and waited there. I took in the smells of the room. Musty and dirty, like unwashed clothes. The acrid aroma of cigarette smoke. But there was something else—some smell I knew as my own.

When the snoring resumed, I made my way to the sofa with excruciating slowness. The light from outside fell directly on the face of the man lying there, and I saw a thick blond beard, a long thin face. This man was not me. He was nothing like me. Which meant the man who was me would be in a bedroom. In the short hallway I first found the bathroom and then felt my way further along to the second door.

I stepped into this room, and right away I sensed the presence of myself asleep on the bed. Walking with confidence now—I had always been a heavy sleeper—I made my way to the side of the bed. This room was dark—I could never tolerate sleeping with any light—so I could not make out the face of the man on the bed whom I knew to be me. But of course I must see him.

Must see myself.

I removed my phone from my pocket and tapped the screen to life. When I directed the light at the bed, there I was. I slept on my right side, legs tucked up and hands at my chest, as I still do. I was sure I was asleep, my chest was rising and falling rapidly, and it occurred to me that this younger self was dreaming.

Was it a dream I had already had or one I would never know?

The me on the bed started and turned away, his breath catching for a moment. I covered my screen, but I saw right away that there was no need. It was merely some disturbance of the dream. I crouched beside him then, moving close enough that I could smell the reek of my own breath. It was distasteful but I did not turn away. I could not turn away. There I lay at arm's length, my smooth hands tucked up under my chin. My hair thick and wavy with the slightest sheen of grease visible in the light from my phone.

It was like watching my own son sleeping, that's what came to me in the bedroom of this stranger who was most assuredly me. But as I squatted there long enough to wake my phone twice, three times, four times, five times, I began to feel something stranger still. I began to feel not as if it was my own son sleeping there beside me, but as if it were, in fact, the real me lying there on the bed. I knew the feel of that face, and had probably spent longer looking at it than I had at my current face.

It seems wrong to admit it, but I felt a small surge of adrenaline at the sight of my younger self sleeping away so innocently. Did I not have enough sense to know that someone had snuck into my room and was right this very moment staring at me with a perverse longing to steal from me that which he could never take? Perhaps the me on the bed had in fact found his way to something like the same thought, because now his breathing altered. It grew shallower and I understood that this younger me might wake. I came to my feet then, shifting the light of my phone to the floor. As I did, it fell on the red flannel jacket that had been discarded. Not thinking, I leaned down to pick it up.

Jacket in hand, I groped in the empty space of the bathroom doorway, stumbled forward and sat on the toilet seat, my heart racing. I held the flannel jacket up to my face, breathed in deeply. It smelt of cotton and cigarettes and, more faintly, my own sweat. I held it against my face until I had to move it aside to breathe, and then leaned backwards with this strangely familiar bundle in my arms.

On the flight home from Invercargill, the cloud cover was impenetrable for the whole journey. An older man sat beside me, reading, and I had a book open on my tray table as well. Only I found it impossible to concentrate. I couldn't get that morning out of my head, and now I'm certain that I never shall.

I had woken to the sound of church bells—in fact a phone alarm, but this was not immediately evident at the time. Before I could recall where I was, I heard footsteps in the small house and I saw someone rushing past the open doorway of the bathroom where I had fallen asleep. Even from a passing glimpse of the figure, I recognised him as the younger me.

I looked around. I was sitting in a small bathroom: shower on one side of me, basin on the other. Panic welled, and I heard the younger me speaking in the other room. His voice didn't exactly sound like mine—the accent was different—and yet there was no denying that this was my voice. It had the same resonance and pitch as mine, the same nasal tone, and, hearing it, I had that awkward feeling I do whenever I listen to a recording of myself.

This voice that was mine was telling the man I'd seen sleeping on the sofa to wake up.

'C'mon, Mike,' the younger me was saying. 'Get the fuck up! We're gonna be late.'

I heard another voice say something I couldn't make out.

'No, you're not, mate,' I said in the other room. 'I'm going to have a shower. By the time I'm done, you better fucking be up!'

I heard footsteps again and, without a thought, rushed for the door of the airing cupboard that I hadn't known was there until that moment. The space behind it was mostly occupied by a large hot water tank, but I squeezed next to it and pulled the door closed. The light flickered on and the door came to a rest, unlatched, against the frame. I saw feet—my own bare feet!—standing on the other side of the airing cupboard door. As I crouched there, the younger me began peeing into the toilet.

I crouched in the small dark space, my face growing hot from the heat of the water tank, as I heard myself turn on the shower. I saw my clothes fall to the floor in a heap and then the feet disappeared. It occurred to me that I might have the briefest window in which to escape, and I had just adjusted my weight to stand when I saw another pair of bare feet enter the bathroom.

It was the other man, Mike. Now Mike began to pee, and I heard myself call from the shower, 'Don't flush! You hear me? Don't fucking flush!'

In the next instant the toilet flushed and the me in the shower cried out. 'You fucking bastard! You're an arsehole, Mike!'

Sitting on the plane later I recalled the excruciating time I spent crouched in that airing cupboard. Despite the fact that the younger me had been insistent that they had to hurry, I was in there for an hour and half, my leg cramping, sweat pouring down my chest, while the two of them talked, ate and then indulged in twenty minutes of video games in the lounge. When at last I heard them putting on their shoes and preparing to leave, I was close to calling out in frustration.

Finally, the front door opened, but when it did I heard the younger me exclaim.

'Holy shit—it's freezing! Let me get my jacket.'

His footsteps passed the bathroom and, on the other side of the wall directly behind me, I listened to him opening a cupboard and muttering to himself. It wasn't until Mike came down the hall to join him and told him they really had to go that it occurred to me what I held in my arms.

The plane continued through the thick cover of grey cloud, and all I could think about was the red flannel jacket in my suitcase. I recalled how I had carefully folded it and tucked it away less than an hour after I had emerged from the airing cupboard that morning and looked out the bathroom window, and I wondered how I could have just stood there and watched myself head off across a snow-whitened lawn, marching away into the cold without my jacket.

HELEN YONG

The Mirror

after Mark Tredinnick

Habits exist that touch the wings of a want
that aches. You're lost in toil but somehow inside is light
setting the shaft of that bone, so you heal
those days when pain was a cage whose bars
doubled as a mirror of self.

This week, seven segments of a new season
have brought the heaviness of early dew
but today sunlight stretches into flight
like the silver body of the jetliner, sliding through
translucence beyond the distant birch tree. It is autumn here
for all living things, while for my far-off friend
the bulbs and blossom, birds and other creatures, shift
into spring. My ulna's long-healed now yet carries
the memory of that winter, snowfalls drifting
deep, and then incessant rain.

KERRY HINES

Thirteen Ways

[A report indicates only 30 per cent of British children can recognise a magpie, but 90 per cent can recognise a Dalek]

i
Among twenty dead planets,
The only moving thing
Was the telescoped eye of the Dalek.

ii
I was of one mind,
Like a world
In which there are innumerable Daleks.

iii
The Dalek swivelled in the autumn winds.
It did not feel wind or Dalek.

iv
A man and a woman
Are nothing.
A man and a woman and a Dalek
Is not a thing.

v
What I prefer does not matter.
I am not on Facebook.
My likes and dislikes
Go unremarked, as though
Pre-exterminated.

vi
Sand drifted up the holiday street, where
Coin-operated machines
Pretended to be Daleks. Inside,
You could spin left or right, proclaiming
Your Dalekhood or keeping silent.
The atmosphere was oppressive. Clouds
Like candyfloss stuck to the sky.

vii
O people of Britain,
How do you imagine you are individuals?
Do you not see that the voices of Twitter
Are Dalek, not magpie, thrush
Or blackbird?

viii
I know grating cadences
And illogical, authoritarian order;
And I know
That the Dalek is implicated
In what I don't know.

ix
When a Dalek floated up a staircase,
It signalled the passing
Of a generation's way out.

x
At the sight of Daleks
Massing in a control room,
Even a child who did not recognise Daleks
Might hold its tongue.

xi
He rode over the Earth
On a horse of the Apocalypse.
Often, he was enveloped in regret
That he would never be
Recognised out of that damned
Dalek suit.

xii
The Earth is moving.
The Daleks are unmoved.

xiii
It was Dalek all Dalek.
It was Dalek
And it was going to Dalek.
The Dalek sat
Dalek.

THERESE LLOYD

Earth Day

The earth rejects all my best notions
so instead, I embrace the air it travels through.
I've seen miles and miles
sliding silver and creamy across the bland circumference
of a passive-aggressive smile.
And there's always more space,
plenty more to fuck up, plenty more to lose.

I have no right to make grand pronouncements
when my day yesterday
was all white chocolate toffee-pops
and napping cat videos.
I have no right to drag
this invisible orb around with me
like a cream donut I'm protecting
by putting it in Tupperware inside my oversized bag,
you know I can't forget it's there
but it's getting bashed
and misshapen and germs are growing
where bits of cream and sugar mate.

JANE ARTHUR

Time-travel TV Series

I watched a German time-travel TV series
because the subtitles meant I could watch it
with the sound off, and like so many things
it went downhill. Not drastically, just a little slip
of its feet on a muddy track. Some parts of life
are too big to put into words. I used to buy
NW magazines and read them sweating on my sofa,
eating apples with sticky fingers and wrists,
giant plums in summer, cumin smell in my armpits,
cracks in the corners of my mouth. And I was often
very cold. The kitchen windows were frosted and once
I pulled my jeans on next to them before opening the door
and it wasn't Matthew, it was my neighbour. I have so much
I've been meaning to tell you. This must have been '07 or '08,
and the cat refused to stay inside after being fixed.
He bashed on the locked catdoor for three hours until
I opened it to let him out and he was fine. He'd eat
a dozen cicadas a day back then. He wasn't a lap cat and
had a short temper but he was loyal and a real beauty
until the sudden tumour in his cheek.
Do I have anything to say? Yes, but it depends
on the timing and it hasn't arrived or it's long passed
or in another dimension I've already come clean.

ANGELA TROLOVE

Study of Lizards

I left that question behind, years ago
'Why do birds chirp?'
Yet it is the only question of all time.

To personify other things
is to transgress a boundary; reflexively, to humanise myself.

I hope the many lizards eat the many ants.
Their tails are a slipstream of their will
a little heart
beats behind the elbow, a reflex in the abdomen
they cast their heads around

tiny sanded crocodiles
a little paunch above the recesses to the rear legs
touchy sunbathers
capsules of agility
ample toes and miniature fingers
marks denoting surface
marks denoting sides and undersurface
the sensation of rock heat
as opposed to the sensation of plant heat

what is lizard heaven? lizard fear?
do they not feel themselves at night,
without this savory anesthetic of sun?
To vanish and to reappear is new entrant
open spreads of absorption
sensual reptiles
flighty and arrested

with this brain I can form the subjunctive perfect
with that brain I could attend
the minerals beneath me
the weight of my tail when I fall
that thing we call instinct
the feeding shapes, their movements
the predator shapes, a course traversed,
and my relatives

I'm not in rapport with this lizard
yet
and all leaves have a life of service
for trees that just keep giving trees
I may give a human one day ...
But this is wonderful!

and that leaf, that sun
their own communion

how to initiate
with an Other?
Proximity, proximity, proximity.
Even for this lifetime.

RENÉ HARRISON

Sightsplain (I)

Brave and flightless
I am all but blind and keep the forest clean
O when will the tūī grant me equity?
Blowing the pūtātara to call Tane back
from ruffled dawn over sheltering flax?
Will only the tuatara remember my courage,
while the fantails laugh
and pūkekos forage?

The sun moves so fast, tongue
tattooing my path,
darting through the nets that Maui cast
I follow the shadow of my beak like a staff.

JESS MACKENZIE

Precise Edges

When my husband left me, I cut him out of every physical photograph I had. I took the little pair of red-handled scissors from my daughter's pencil case and cut carefully around his image. There was something gratifying about it, real, definitive, those metal blades slicing through that thick glossy paper, and the final clip as the two blades joined together again.

It was a premeditated crime with purpose, revenge that mixed catharsis with concentration. I could have screwed the pictures up, burned them, even simply torn them and left a ragged edge between us, but instead I took the time to sit and remove him from each photograph, from the moments of my life that had been worth capturing.

I left the background, the setting, even the plot. But I removed him to the very last shadow of hair. He was just a shape filled with space, that for twelve years had played a role in my life. But, ultimately, he could have been anyone.

When he left, he took my daughter. They gave him my daughter. That's not usually how it goes, but they foresaw potential instability from my work. I'm a marine biologist. I need to travel for my job, and I spend a lot of time in the ocean.

The ocean is vast and deep. It's uncharted. Despite everything, we're still confined to the surface and still know only a handful of its creatures, the bare minimum of its secrets. The darkness begins at 1000 metres and stretches farther than we can travel unassisted. We don't know what's down there, in those spaces. It could be anything.

That's no place to take a child.

At first I saw her just once a month, but I worked hard to prove myself, that I could be there, be present. I juggled my work and made my schedule more predictable. I proved that I was more than just anyone.

One evening my daughter ran away from my husband's new house and showed up at my door. My eight-year-old daughter crossed the dark streets just to see me. It was late and I'd stepped out the back for a smoke, then taken myself for a walk around the block. The gate was cold under my hand and the sky was boundless, with fragments of light suspended in the dark.

When I came back she had found her way through the unlocked door and was sitting in the pool of lamplight by the coffee table, holding a pile of cut photographs.

She'd gathered them from around the house and placed them about her, all those images I'd sliced with precision and redistributed to their old places. She had frames and plastic sheaths, raw photos, even the scrapbooks I'd glued back together.

The light showed the tear streaks on her cheeks in silver, and I'll never forget her face when she looked at me. It was hurt. It was as simple and plain, as deep, as that.

I don't know why she decided she still wanted to stay that night, but she did, in the little single bed in the room that had always been hers. I warmed milk for her and filled up a hot-water bottle. She pushed it to the bottom of her bed with her feet to keep her toes warm.

In the morning I went to the kitchen to make a coffee. On the bench were three of my favourite books about marine mammals and cartilaginous fish. They were open, butchered, the sea creatures cut out precisely. I could read the words on the opposite page through the outlines of porpoises and skates.

A pain cut through my chest and rose to the surface. I made a small noise.

I could hear my daughter in the living room. She was sitting on the sofa with pillows arranged around her like a nest, quietly drawing on a notepad as if nothing was wrong.

When she saw me, she began scribbling with the felt-tip pen, pressing it into the paper. I walked across and stood in front of her with my arms folded. Whatever she'd been drawing was obscured in a whirlpool of dark lines that started at the edges of the page and circled inwards, tight and heavy, to the centre.

She put her pen down in the middle of the page and looked up at me. There was a smudge of black ink on her lower lip. On the couch next to her lay the little red-handled scissors.

I picked them up and asked her what she thought she was doing.

She looked back at me, her dark eyes expressionless. The pen rolled off her page and bounced on the floor.

I asked her again, holding the scissors out in front of me like punctuation.

She said nothing, but suddenly launched herself off the sofa and ran past me, scattering the contents of her pencil case and sending her defaced drawings flying. She slammed her bedroom door. A picture fell off the wall onto the hallway carpet with a thud.

I stood with the scissors clutched tight in my hand, looking at the mess of pages, the overturned pillows, the small empty space my daughter had left on the sofa.

MICHAEL MINTROM

Flickering Between Shadow and Light

Philip Clairmont's Paintings—Five Responses

1.
Stench-laden, ferocious nor'west wind,
You've blown for days. Crazed
Farm people, new migrants to town,
Arrive with you upon their backs,
Blood in their shoes, jackets full of dust.
Under your influence, my mind's
Become a wheeling clothesline.
Both day and night, the ancient
Contraption twists and turns.
My thoughts are paint-daubed rags.

2.
The room's walls are radiant scarlet,
As if we've entered a human skull.
Below an awkwardly hanging mirror,
The couch, once elegant, erupts.
We witness the metamorphosis—
Flailing plant turning to rough beast.
The couch is primed for vengeance.
Long it suffered naked oppression
Under splendid imperialist bottoms.
Shortly, it will arise—the screaming führer.

3.
The nightmare starts under a yellow bulb.
You are drawn up bare wooden stairs,

Flickering between shadow and light.
Through baroque arches, you step
Alongside the rooms of the dead.
The mirror reveals your distorted face:
Your eyes stare back from a mask of ash.
The swastika appears, black and blue.
Torn body parts of those you hid,
Even from yourself, ooze out to meet you.

4.
The fireplace looms like a theatre's stage.
When I observe closely the flames,
They exude a terror-twisted beauty.
The scene transports me to Europe
And the wars. The conflagration will spare
Nothing. All orange and yellow, the fire
Tears through buildings, turns day to night.
The innocent and the damned, tossed
Together in one last struggle, fight
The fire storm's suck—and succumb to it.

5.
Jazz saxophone played through the night.
Lazarus appeared to me. Centuries before,
From the desert's edge, his sister sent
Word for the Holy One. In my wardrobe,
Half-skeletal, worm-eaten, there he hung,
Breathing. Even now, his pungent stink
Clings to my dungarees. Those presumed
Dead are with me, drifting among the living.
When the pageant arrives, come join me.
I paint in the crack between life and death.

LISSA MOORE

Untitled

Ask me where we began and I'll remember
the apple trees dipping in rows to the river,
wooden crates stacked empty
waiting by the open barn doors,
the soft yip of a little owl in the copse
on the hill, dew starting
and stars like blossom in the branches.

I'll remember how night fell rosy-green,
the edge of summer, a close-coming
ripeness in the air, your skin
and the two of us meeting like wings
leaving the bed of the orchard below.

DAVID GREGORY

The Folding Map

His hand smoothed,
his finger traced
the broken course of ships;
wave, trough, wave,
dotted around the Horn.
The broken course of love,
the relief of *pushing off
from the land*,
How the sea breaks,
merciful and merciless.

Now his voyage is
two streets from home:
step, shuffle, step,
newspaper, milk and
on the last corner,
between high-rises,
a shuttered view of sea.

He searches for his ships
in so many bottles.

JESSICA LE BAS

The White Chairs

Those to whom the gods/Grant nothing are free ... —Ricardo Reis, 1934

He wrote about 'nothing' like it was a product
He stacked it in verses, shelves, like at Pak'nSave, say

or CITC at Avarua. Nothing comes without
the boat each month from Auckland. No petrol
for three days. We stayed home. Waited

waited like the horizon waits. The Pacific Ocean,
its tight-lipped line drawn above the reef

Nothing here needs explanation

The spinning of this circular island, so fast
that bits flew off—some to the north where
nothing much else appears. In the south

the debris bore islands, with strings attached
by air currents, and a flight schedule at AirRaro

All is nothing and there is plenty for all

In the heat that pulls the pawpaw to the sky
The flat hands lifted to the heavens

In a lagoon the colour of the spinning tern
We see ourselves on the other side

And in the black pearls sold as souvenirs
Warriors carved in their blue-bellied shells

And yes, in the songs Mama Anna sings
with children, in their bright shirts, giving thanks,
blessing the white plastic chairs
that arrive on the barge.

IAIN TWIDDY

The Catch

Orua morning, the blue bay glooping,
the sea a dazzling mirror of the sky;
rowing the boat's dented shell through the cross-tide
back to the bach, where the car doors thudded,
the women and kids down from the farm for lunch.

It was the first time I'd caught a real fish.
The first time the line slicing the belly
had twanged, and triggered that one-shot up-prick,
the yank-back—like uprooting a sapling—
the first time the upflurried blue had smoothed

into the pink of dragon wings, the rip-
lipped, fan-backed gurnard, pliered off the hook
into the shallow scratch of the bucket,
in which he lashed and bellowed like a toad
for an hour under the pulverant sun.

When the boat had scrunched up the beach, before
we went up, I was told *Stick your finger
in his mouth, you can carry him that way.*
I must've blanched or looked up, but Wayne said
Don't worry about him mate, he's fucked.

So I did. And still in my fingertips
feel the flinch as my finger wormed its way in,
past the tingling milky ridges of him
who, though doomed, had hooted, boomed and thrashed, more
of a fish than I had yet been a man.

JAMES NORCLIFFE

Naughty Boys' Island

Not so much an island:
more a grey sandbank
dividing a grey river where
it broadened out between
lines of pollarded tamarisks
just before Brighton.

You had always lived there:
dreamt of crouching among
the reeds, the debris,
the silt-stained plastic bags
and broken bottles, of claiming
your muddy citizenship,

although you were never as
naughty as the river that
wet your stolen cigarettes,
extinguished your matches.
Let me take you to my island
the wicked river whispered.

*I'll be waiting here for you when
you have coined those fucking cars,
kicked those letterboxes over*
the wicked river lied.
*Trust my channels, trust
my current, trust my rushing tide.*

SUSAN TE KAHURANGI KING

This Awakening/Tēnei Ohonga Ake

1. Untitled, graphite, coloured pencil and crayon on paper, 430 x 300 mm.
2. Untitled, graphite, coloured pencil and crayon on paper, 297 x 210 mm.
3. Untitled, graphite, coloured pencil and crayon on paper, 335 x 210 mm.
4. Untitled, graphite and crayon on paper, 335 x 207 mm.
5. Untitled, graphite, coloured pencil and crayon on paper, 335 x 210 mm.
6. Untitled, graphite and crayon on paper, 285 x 302 mm.
7. Untitled, graphite, coloured pencil and crayon on paper, 265 x 160 mm.
8. Untitled, graphite, crayon and gouache on paper, 200 x 200 mm.

All images c. 1975–80. Courtesy of the artist, Robert Heald Gallery (Wellington) and Chris Byrne (Dallas, US).

Perky, wildly surreal, fascinated by pattern and the emotionally suggestive powers of simple cartooning, Susan Te Kahurangi King's vision roams from jointed doll-like figures and Looney Tunes characters to the rhythmic potential in geometric mosaic. Muted, ashen graphite is peppered with bursts of primary colour. With a similar sense of contrast, blank space sculpts out a stillness deep within a bustle of images. The intriguing interplay between blank canvas and visual hubbub seems evocative of silence, fallowness, depression, absence or the abyss and their opposites: creative surge, the proliferation of forms and possibilities; the crescendo of chase scenes or the slapstick humour of old Saturday morning cartoons; perhaps even city crowds, social jostle. The recycled or 'repurposed' paper in many of the works implies the busy family context they were made in; yet also creative urgency, spontaneity and determination.

Reminiscent of children's optical puzzles, in some works here, the longer you search, the more figures appear in the burgeoning field of tessellations. Once you discover these figures, the subtleties of facial expression, even in the apparently guileless cartoons, range from intimations of cruelty and slyness to melancholia and introspection, mischief or jubilation. Te Kahurangi King's work can make us want to alter Samuel Johnson's famous line about London and apply it to this artist: 'There is in Susan all that life can afford.' —Emma Neale. Thanks to Karyn Paringatai

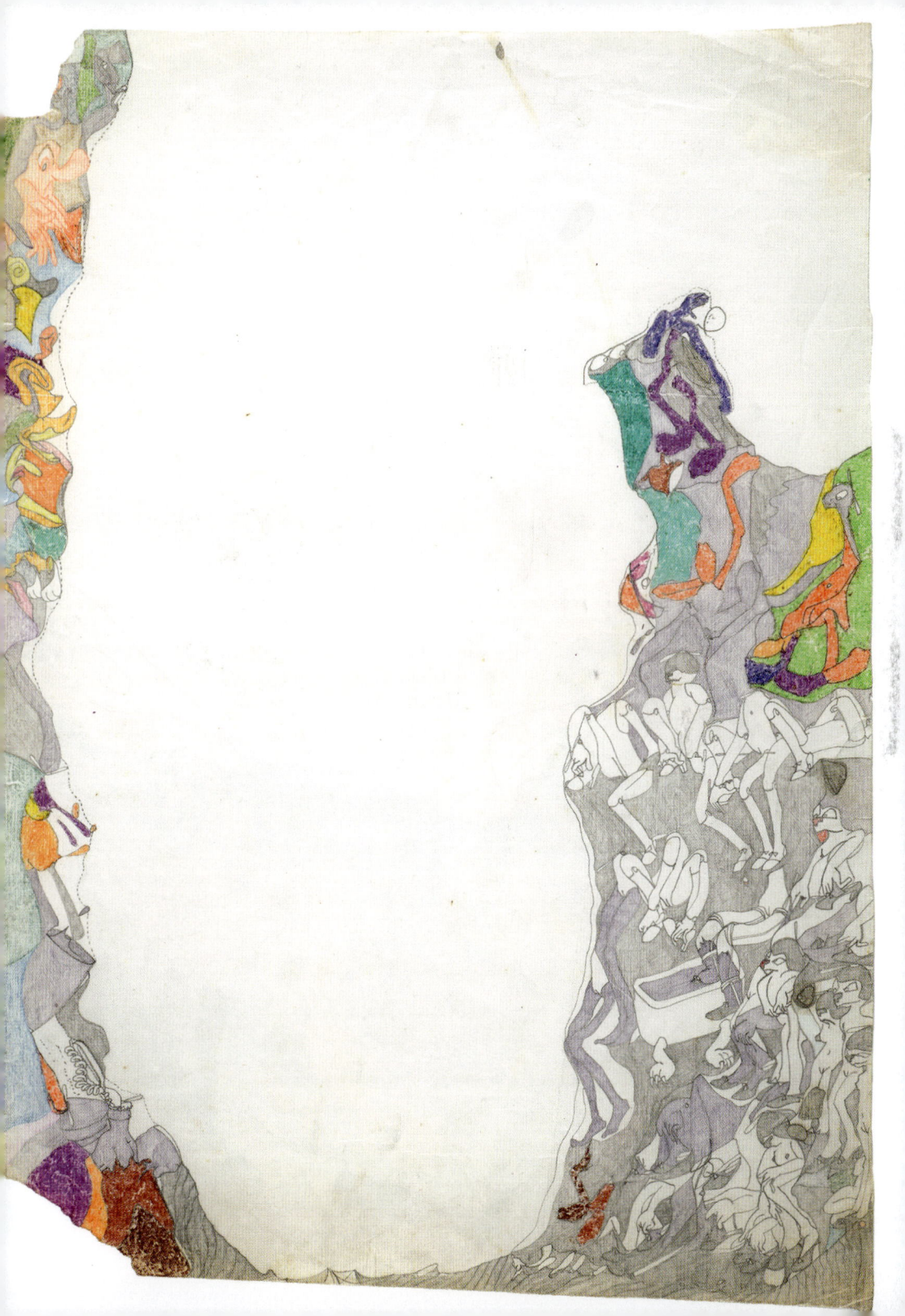

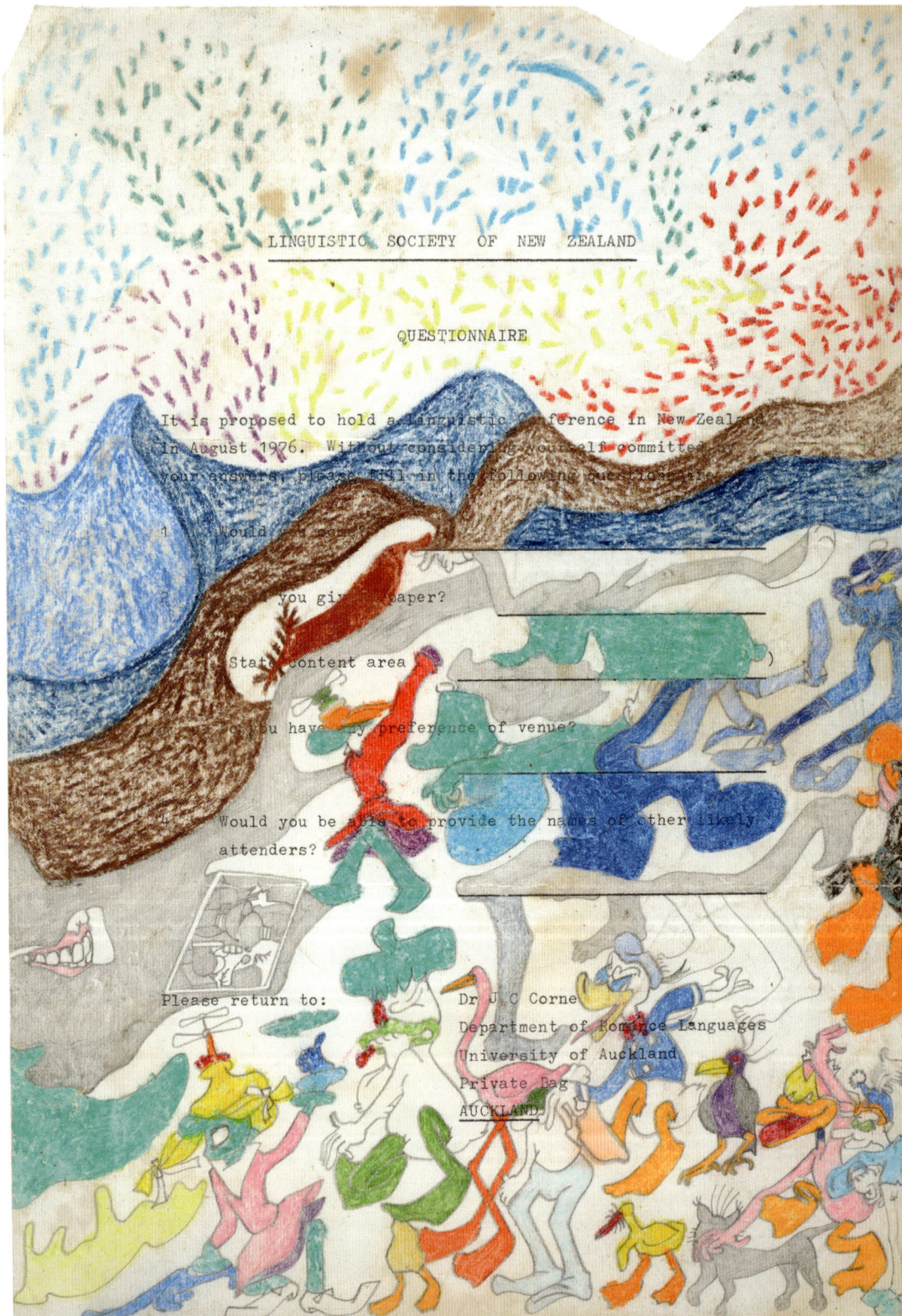

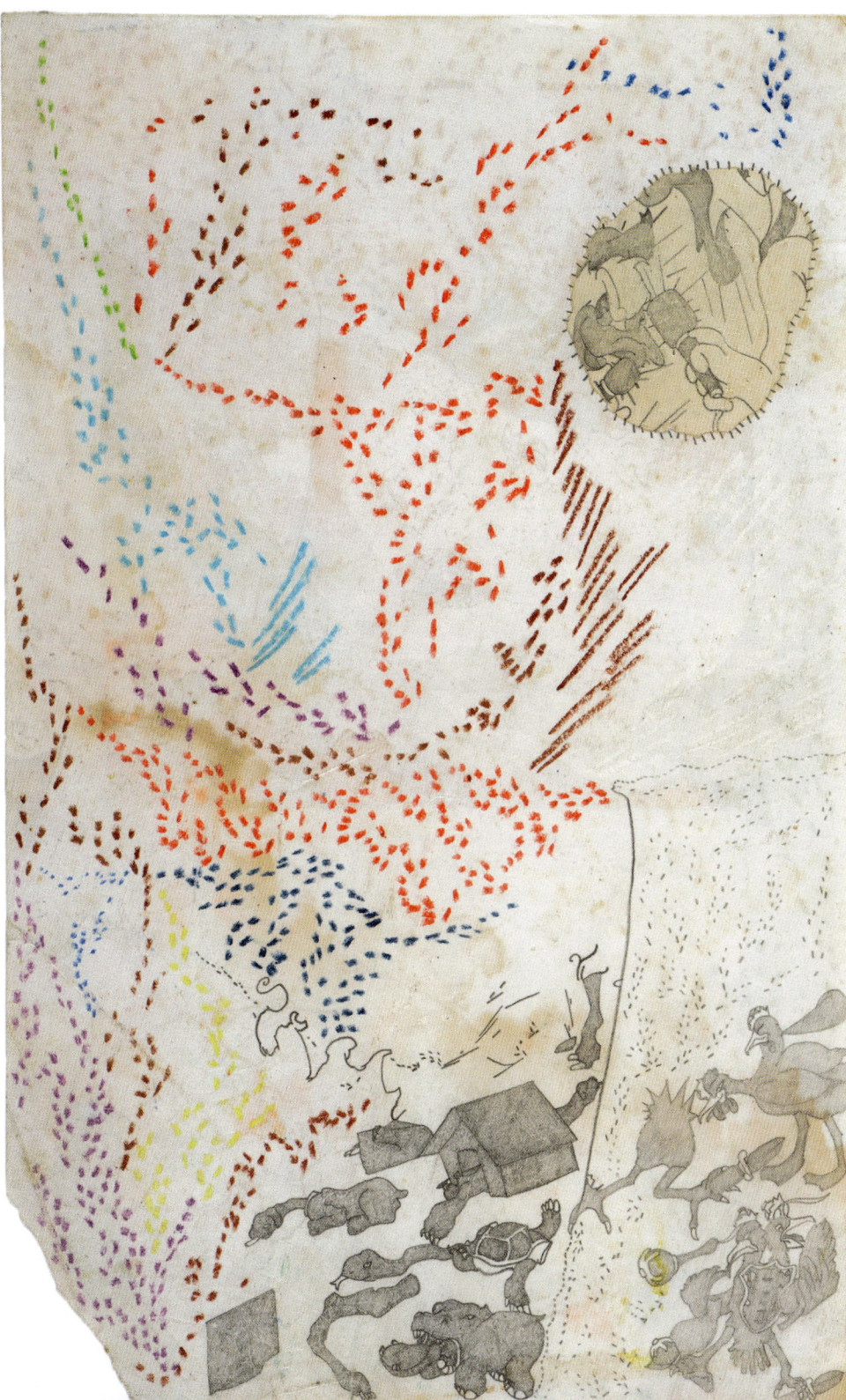

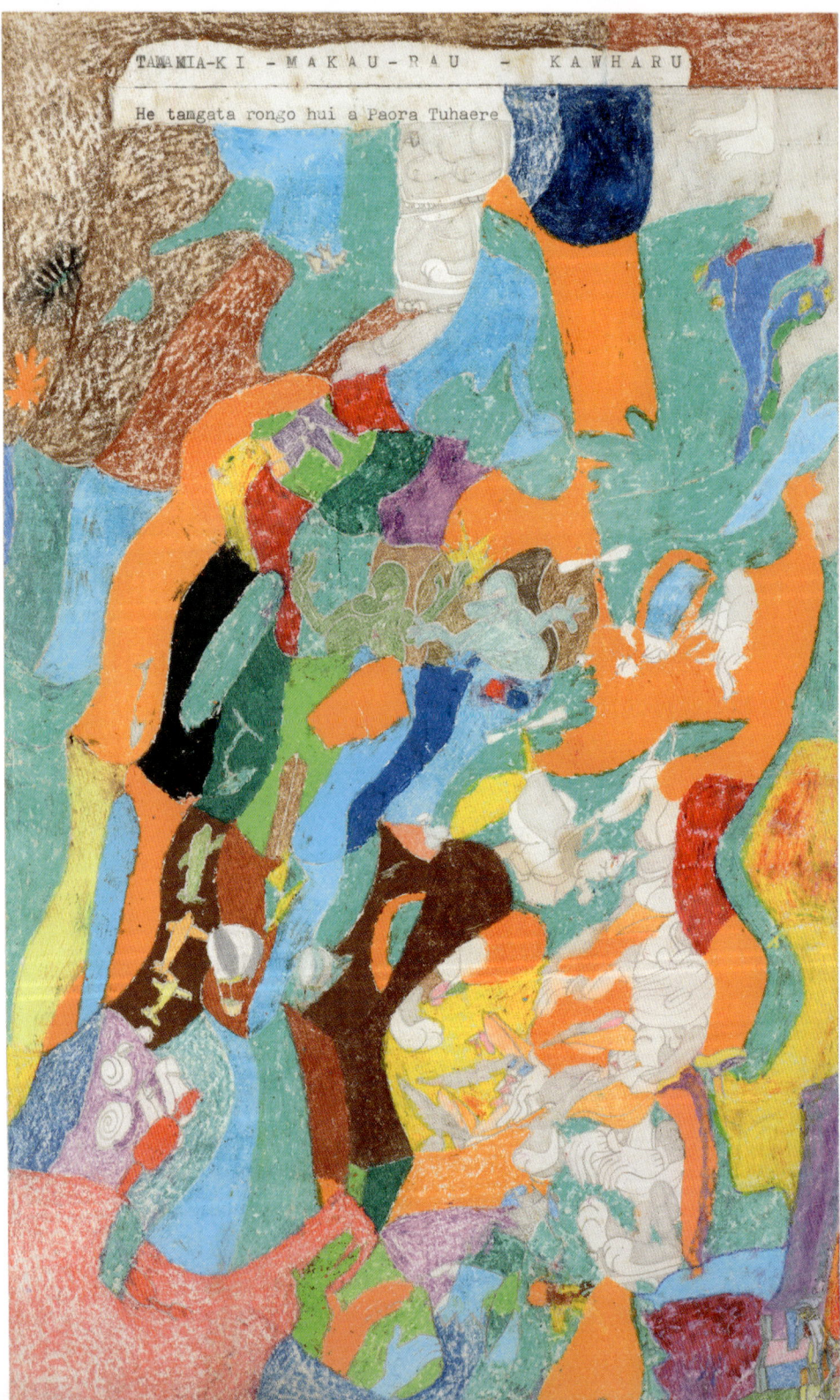

TAMAKI-KI - MAKAU-RAU - KAWHARU

He tangata rongo hui a Paora Tuhaere

QUESTIONNAIRE

Name: Maori Class Name:

Address:

Age: A if 21 or over;   Phones (home)   ; (bus)
      age if under 21.
                         Occupation:

Adult Evening Class Course (Language and Culture) - BASIC MAORI
                                                    ADVANCED MAORI

School: Year:

Previous linguistic studies or experience.
   MAORI:

   OTHER LANGUAGES:

Are you trying to learn another language concurrently with Maori?

Motive for learning Maori:

Practical application of Maori studies:

Current hobbies, studies or other interests:

What influenced you to enrol in this course:

TAPE RECORDER (tick here as applicable):
   I have a tape recorder (reel size   inches, tape speeds   ).
   I intend acquiring one (reel size   inches, tape speeds   ).
   I could have the use of a tape recorder.

ATTENDANCE: Do you know of any reason which would prevent regular attendance through the whole year. If so, please state.

HOMEWORK: Are you prepared to do the minimum prescribed homework throughout the course?

GENERAL REMARKS:

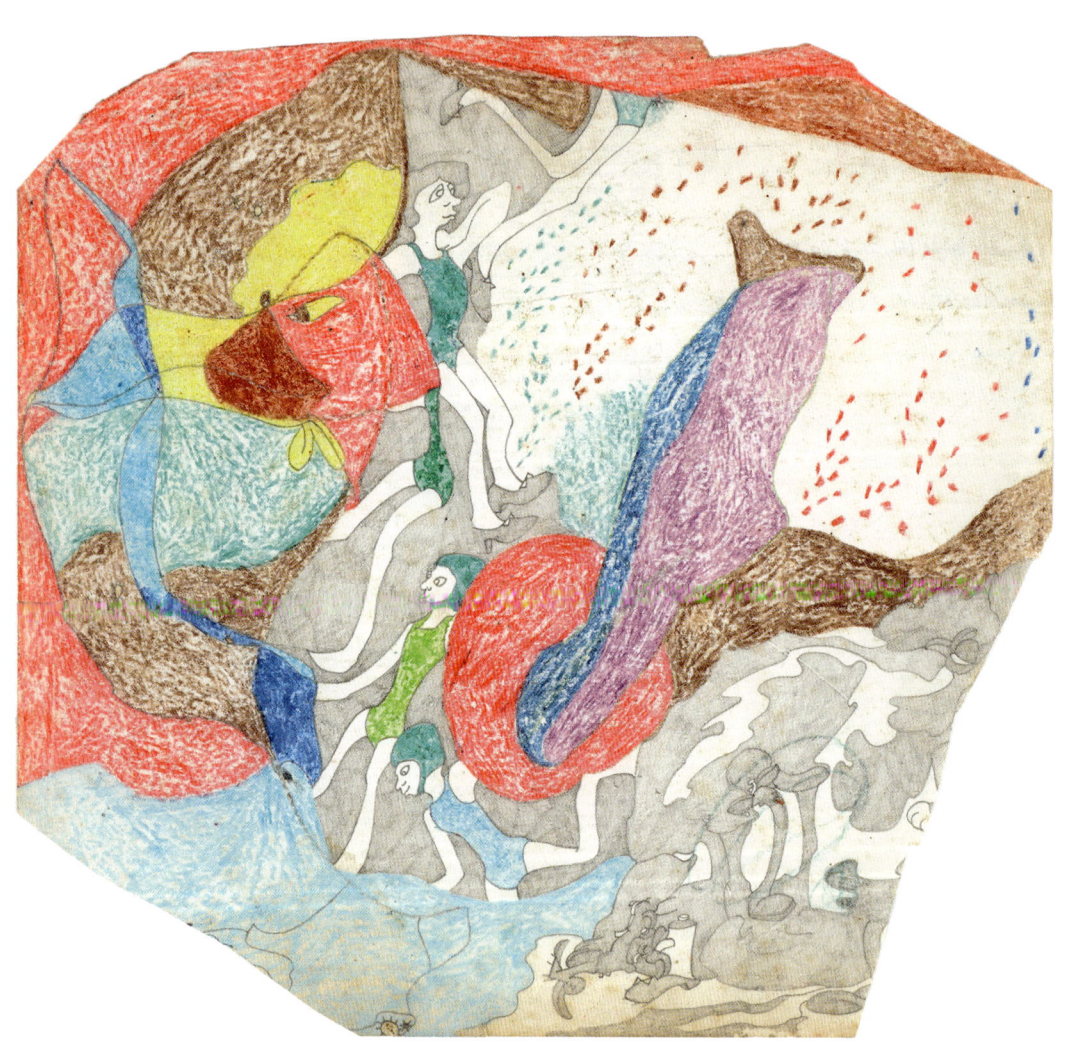

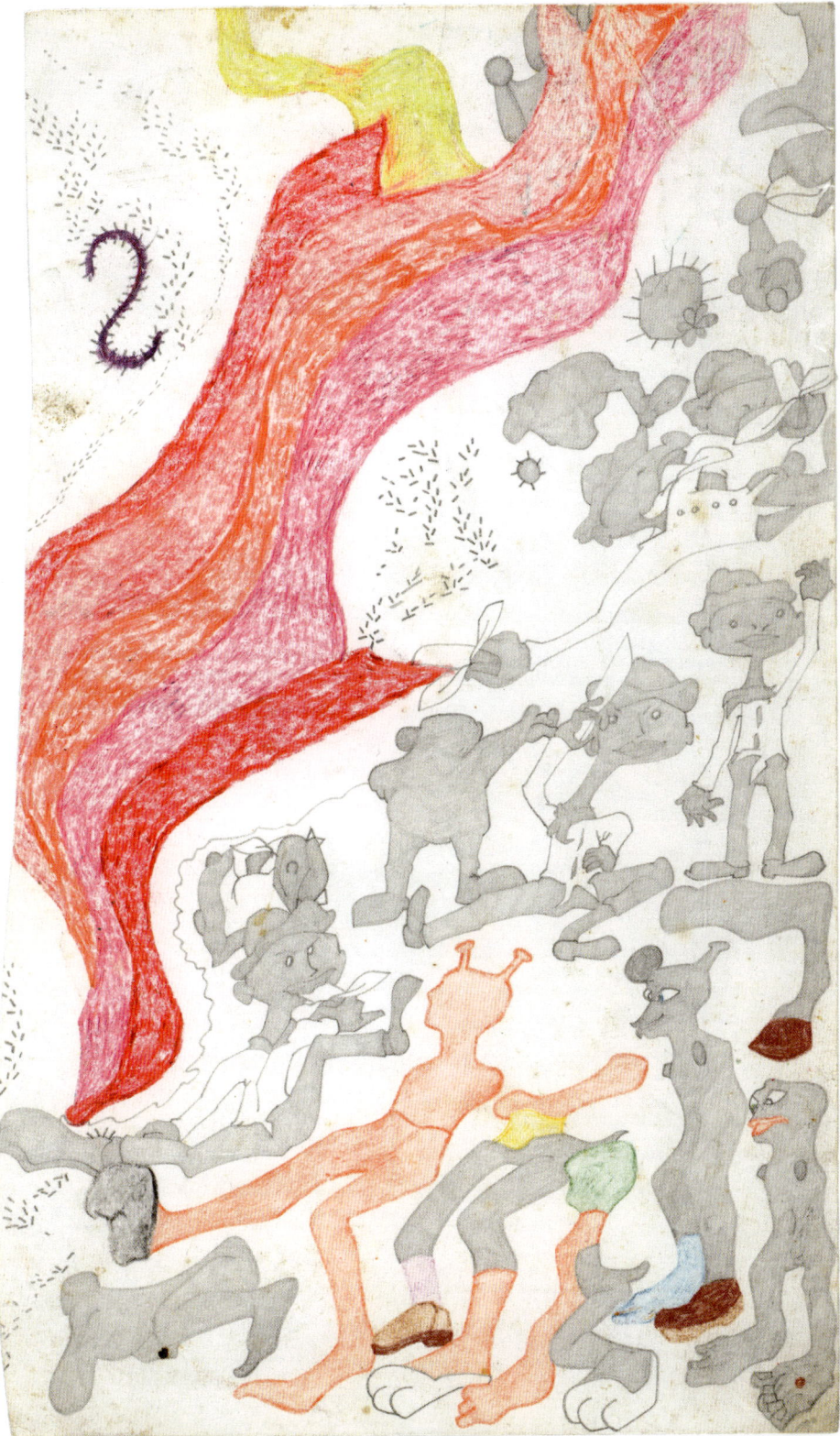

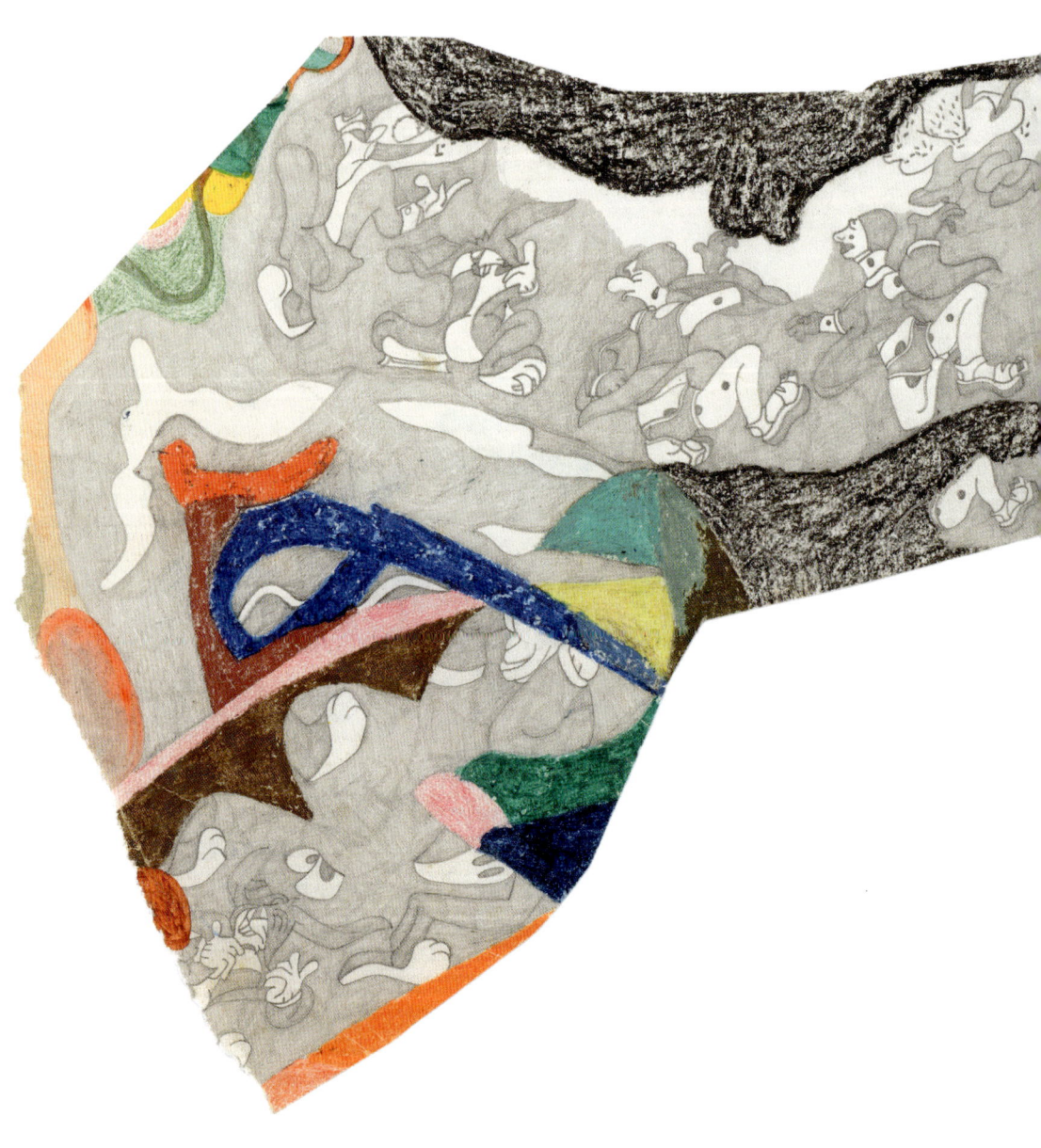

BRETON DUKES

Hector

It's been raining and the ditch to the side of the gravel track is muddy and puddled. Hector's wearing gumboots and green and blue overalls and now he sits and heels himself, feet first, down the bank, into a puddle.

'Puddle,' he says, stomping.

I crouch to be close in case of a problem, looking up and down the track. This place is popular with dog-walkers and, probably because of my own fear, I'm scared of big dogs coming in fast and scaring Hector (or worse) with big teeth and jaws.

He dips the rice cracker he's holding into puddle-water and takes a bite.

'Uh uh, no,' I say.

He chews, looking at me, and feints to dip again.

'C'mon,' I say. 'Not that. No, Hector.'

He stops—on his terms—and climbs out of the ditch and up the bank where he kicks into the gravel, squats to finger it, then stands and says, 'Run, Daddy.'

My knees are old. These days in order to keep the weight out of them I mince rather than run. So that's what I do, mince up the path, and that's more than enough for Hector who, getting going, getting his little arms working, runs, smiling up at me.

'Daddy's running.'

'I am,' I say, winding my own arms and gaping comically.

'Stop,' he says, so I do. 'Go,' he says, so I do.

And in this way we get past the soccer field that makes the other side of the track and up to a place where there's a two-metre drop to the Kaikorai Stream, where black water falls, making a white mat of bubbles.

'Blankie,' says Hector.

'It's back in the car, old mate,' I say. 'Blankie's in the car.'

Crouched again, I've got him between my knees with my hands around his stomach, which goes out and in with his breath.

'Like blankie,' he says pointing, and I see what he means. The bubbling white water, the form of it, looks like his comforter.

'Yes,' I say, 'it is like blankie.'

Knowing this already, he doesn't respond.

He's 27 months, and wears pull-ups for active boys weighing between 13 and 18 kilograms. He's into baked beans, gurnard, plates of oven fries, ice-cream and dancing. He dances in our bedroom and the lounge; he dances with my old tennis racquet, checking his form in the reflection made in our sliding doors; he strums and bobs and shifts from one foot to the other. Or for a whole song he'll just jump. Jump, play his guitar, hiccup and laugh.

Back where our car is parked, past the soccer field, there is the sound of car doors shutting.

'What's that noise?' says Hector.

'A car,' I say, picking up a small stone and lobbing it into the water. 'Plop,' I say, close to his ear.

But he's watching the carpark. Two people stand by an old ute. A white dog squats by the bin other dog-walkers use for the tied-off little baggies they've used for their animal's shit.

'C'mon,' I say, 'let's run.'

I start to wheel away, but Hector, though he's stood, is still facing the dog and the people.

I'm in shorts, but also a puffer jacket. Hector's in a pirate's hat—the shape of Napoleon's—with a lamb's-wool tunic over his overalls. Size-wise, he's on the seventy-fifth percentile. I was always small. At Otago Boys' High I was puny with an oversized head and ears that stuck out. Occasionally I was bullied.

The occasion I recall most readily was at lunch during a summer inter-school—I played tennis. I was sitting opposite a popular boy who, in the fifth form, was already an all-rounder in the first eleven. We were at big tables, eating rolls filled with lettuce, hardboiled eggs and ham, and drinking from cardboard containers of Just Juice.

'Fucking look at this,' the all-rounder said, nudging the boy beside him, and pointing to me in my pastel and white tennis polo. 'Look at his fucking arms! How can he get the ball over the net?'

Chewing, the other boy had nodded but stayed quiet.

Maybe it was his mate's lack of interest that made the all-rounder mad. 'Ethiopian,' he said, glaring. 'Fucking little Ethi.'

He was tall and broad with a tanned face and a long fringe, and for the rest of the meal he glared and sniggered and kicked me under the table. Actually, I don't remember that. And I don't even know if he was one of the people who called me Ethi. But this was the eighties—the famines were on TV—and I did get called that occasionally.

No doubt we had to stay seated at those plastic trestle tables until a teacher said we could get up. Probably the all-rounder would have lost interest in me and my arms almost immediately. Maybe he'd stuffed around with his juice container, maybe he'd popped it with the heel of his hand or shot the sugary juice out of the straw. Maybe he'd have talked about the state of the game they were playing. But twenty-seven years later I remember sitting there opposite him, so I must have been scared.

'Up,' says Hector, raising his arms, still watching the dog, which is lean and fast and making crazy swoops over the soccer field. I pick Hector up and walk. He's got his legs either side of my hip and his hand around my neck and he pushes his face into the wind like I'm a horse he's riding one-handed. I'm glad he's big. I don't want him to be a bully, but I don't want him scared. I want him to be open and strong and quick to laugh. I want him to be known for his loud shirts and loud laugh. I want him to be into eye-popping recreations like kite-surfing or base-jumping. I want him drumming in a rock band and driving a convertible. I want him to be one of those people you think about when they're not around—a person of such presence, that, in wondering where they are, you also feel envy for those lucky enough to be close to them.

He's twisted and is looking back down the track. 'What's that?' he says.

I turn. Now the dog's down drinking in the ditch. On the path above, there's a man in a woollen hat, and a woman. 'A dog, a thirsty doggy,' I say, wanting to sound casual, not wanting any anxiety crossing over. Wanting to be a father who can deal with dangerous dogs with a loud voice or a well-timed kick.

Hector swivels again and I bump his ear with my cheek. His ears are soft, but not squishy. The cartilage shape of them is firm but pliable, and the delicate edge is cool against my cheek.

Ahead the bush closes a little on either side of the track. Further on it opens again and up there is the woodchip pile I'm aiming to get to.

We go past some low-hanging trees and I dip and dive him through the wet leaves.

'Aaar!' he says. 'Good game!' he says, giggling.

I turn to run him through the leaves again. The dog's gone back to blasting around the soccer field. The man's still on the path, while the woman's out on the field with a lead yelling at the dog.

'Hooper!' she shouts. '*Hooper. Come.*'

The dog doesn't respond, just keeps running. Probably they're trying to get the animal under control before getting too close to us.

Even with all the drinking I've done, all the late nights out, I've never been in a fight. Never stood up for myself or someone else, or defended a vulnerable person, or broken up some beastly act by, say, wrapping my arms around an offender, or crash-tackling some dick. I don't like violence. That's part of it. But the main part is cowardice. When a violent thing happens and the brain is charged with the chemical that imposes either fight or flight, I'll fly. But not if the thing was a person drowning in a river, or if a bedroom was burning up; then, I think, I'd go in. But I'd defend Hector wouldn't I? Or Liz, my wife? I'd fight then?

Hector's getting heavy but I check back down the track before putting him down.

'Let's look for mushrooms,' I say.

He looks up at me. His eyes go wide and he flaps his mouth, 'A, a, a,' he says, sorting through the words in his brain, 'a mushroom hunt.'

'A mushroom hunt,' I confirm.

Ahead, I can see the woodchips. Beside the track are areas of mown, sloping grass. Beyond that, on our right, the council have planted toetoe and other native plants on a hill that gets steep fast, while on the other side, between the track and the stream, there's a picnic table and then some scruffy bush where we've found mushrooms before.

I look back, but the track's curved slightly and I can't see the people or the dog. I dangle my hand and Hector takes it.

'It's a good walk,' he says.

At his twenty-first, at his wedding, at his child's first birthday, on the day he buys his first house or makes a big impression in some big city, I want to be beside him, elegantly dressed, holding a glass of champagne, saying some wise and funny thing while his good friends/lovers/wife/children smile and raise their drinks as I hold him and tell him I'm proud, that I can't love anything more than I love him.

We cross the grass and he leads me, ducking, into the bush, which is dark and cool and where the sound of the stream is louder.

A year or more after that inter-school lunch the all-rounder was driving the northern motorway late at night with some of the other popular boys when he lost control of the car and hit and killed a woman whose own car had broken down. The all-rounder's brother had been a prefect and maybe dux. His dad had a firm offering financial services for wealthy Dunedinites. After a short time, while he was away from school, there was a court appearance and after that the all-rounder was back and playing again for the first eleven.

'Mushroom,' goes Hector.

I look. 'I think it's a bone,' I say. 'It's a similar colour though isn't it?'

Hector squats and prods. 'Bone,' he says.

I crouch and we investigate. 'Might be from a sheep,' I say.

'Might be,' he says.

'Or a dog—a hyena,' I say, because it's a word he's enjoyed before.

But, 'Hmm,' is all he says, followed by 'woodchips'.

'Shall we go up to the woodchips?' I say.

He looks at me, light coming into his eyes. 'I like chips,' he says, throwing his arms into the air with such gusto his feet leave the ground and he rotates slightly on the spot.

Crouching again, leading the way, I go back out onto the grass. No sign of the dog or the people, but there is barking. I look back at where I've exited the bush, where Hector now comes, stumbling and then tripping and then standing. His pirate hat's fallen low over his eyes, but despite that he starts to walk, tipping his head right back to see.

'I'm sing you a song, Daddy,' he says.

I wait for him and adjust his hat. 'A song?'

'Yeah,' he says, nodding in his serious way, like it's something he's been thinking about for a long time.

'At the woodchips?' I say, taking his hand and heading towards the mound.

'Hmm.'

Again, I look down the path, but the barking's stopped. Maybe the animal and its owners have gone back to the car.

There was my friend Richard. Dick, we called him. Dick killed himself. After university we flatted together in Auckland in a shit-box at the Jervois Road end of John Street in Herne Bay. I was working as a labourer on a building site; he was a junior pharmacist in Kingsland. After work we'd lift weights at a Newton gym and then take benzodiazepine and drink wine cooler. On his OE he got into the medical heroin returned by families of people who'd been using the drug for relieving pain related to terminal cancer. He made it back to Auckland, but later overdosed in his bathroom. Deregistered, he went back to the UK, where he overdosed again and died, aged twenty-five.

The woodchip pile makes a stage a metre off the ground. I'm sat off to the side, looking at Hector who's up there with a toetoe stem, and now he squats, working his bottom hand like it's the strings of a double bass he's playing.

'Oh,' I say, 'yes!'

'Ooh ya,' he says, smiling and bobbing.

I applaud. 'Is that your song? Ooh ya?'

'Ooh ya,' he sings, 'Ooh ya.'

And oh, what a glorious scene. Framed by wet green trees and a blue sky, golden hair in tufts and curls beneath his skull and crossbones. Weeping, I clap and applaud and laugh and he bobbles faster, and in concentrating on getting his voice low or high he sometimes forgets to play the toetoe, just stands tall and thrusts his heart forward, bellowing, and as long as I'm prepared to hoot and yell 'Bravo, encore, encore,' he's happy to set himself for another brief, persuasive, performance.

But then, beyond him, I see the couple. Because Hector's blocking some of the path, I can't see the dog straight away, but when I move a bit, I see it's close, white wolfish jaws so relaxed its teeth clatter lightly as it comes on, undulating.

'Hector,' I say, and straight onto the fear in my voice he stops his song and reaches for me, but though I've said his name urgently my feet are spaghetti, and instead of standing and throwing him onto my shoulders, instead of preparing a defence, I sort of crawl forward and around the woodchips—at least I'm between him and the dog, the dog that's only ten metres away, eye to eye with a skinny, unshaven forty-three-year-old.

'Hooper! Hooper!' goes the woman.

'Daddy!' says Hector.

'Hey!' says the male dog-walker, and so mine is the only brain not vocalising; instead it's got me elbows down on the path, my forehead gravel-bound, my bum raised, so what I am is a ramp for the animal to run and leap and hunt my son's throat. My brain—and what it's learnt of submitting before wild animals from Wilbur Smith and Attenborough documentaries—supplicates my body before this scrawny dog that now skids in, lipping gravel onto my hands, but instead of fangs, or even hot breath, all I feel is a wet nose sniff-sniffing over my bald spot.

And then tongue in my ear. 'Yeah,' I say to the gravel, and finally I reach back for Hector who must have already come off his stage because he finds me first, setting his little hand on my back, and it's this contact that gets me looking up.

'It's okay, it's okay,' says the woman, who's standing there on the path, looking at me shyly, and here's the man, who, same as the dog, has a wrinkled face and a bulging right eye, and he says, 'Hooper likes children, he can't get enough of them.' And so I change from my submissive shape to a more standard, dog-patting crouch, while at the same time gathering Hector close, and after a moment—the animal's dead-still, stunned maybe by the thing it had me do—I get back to being Dad, showing Hector where to scratch and which way to stroke the fur.

'Dog,' says Hector.

'Hooper,' I say, my voice sounding like it's coming through the radio. 'This is Hooper.'

The man—he seems the least thrown by my performance—nods at Hector. 'It's a good day for pirating.' But Hector's shy around men and after staring at him a moment he says to me, 'Up,' and so finally I pick him up, holding him as Hooper—who's also come back to himself—licks the soles of Hector's new blue sneakers.

'All right,' I say, raising my eyebrows at the couple who've moved a little up the path, but then stopped, watching while Hector dangles his hand to Hooper's lapping tongue.

The woman looks at my dusty knees and nods.

I nod too. 'Bye, Hooper,' I say, and start walking back down the track.

In my arms, Hector turns and looks over my shoulder: maybe at the dog, maybe at the friendly man, maybe at the path that becomes a track that leads up to Brockville with its views, wind, bus stops and state houses.

Your son killing someone. Your son killing himself. Neither of those two outcomes would be good for a parent. That's what I am now—a parent.

In summer, at the Logan Park courts, from age ten to sixteen, Dad and I used to play tennis after tea until it got so dark the ball would disappear when you hit it over the net. Dad whose black beard has gone totally silver, who, when he was my age, was divorced and doing the Coast to Coast every year, while his own parents, now dead, were both, I don't know, playing five hundred with their cobbers, say, camping in their huge, pre-World War II tent, eating dinner watching Tom Bradley read the TV news.

When Dad was the age I am now, I was fourteen. I hadn't yet left that John Street flat, hadn't yet left Dick there with all his pills and moved to stay with Grandad in St Martins, Christchurch, where, depressed, and feeling left behind, and feeling pressure to get my own OE started, I forged Grandad's name on one of his cheques, banked five thousand of his dollars, and disappeared to Perth.

I put Hector down and hold his hand. What we'll do is go and buy a popsicle from the Four Square on Kaikorai Valley Road. He'll eat his and then get little bites from mine and then we'll do something with the sticks—draw faces on them or use a rubber band to make aeroplanes.

Adult life: for Hector, it's just a series of days and nights away. And right now is a Sunday, in February 2017, and he's two years three months old. At the moment he's getting used to a new timetable of day care, he's learnt to get in and out of his car seat on his own, he can pull his trousers up (but only at the front), he doesn't know the vacant feeling you get from benzo's, he doesn't know about cigarettes or impotence, or G-strings, he doesn't know that the night before I was flying out to Perth with my stolen money I stayed with Dick and we got drunk, and in the morning I woke up on his kitchen floor, looking at the yolk, white and shell of an egg Dick had dropped when we got home, when he was preparing to cook me one of his famous fried egg/melted cheese sandwiches.

'We'll get a popsicle, eh?' I say.

'I like popsicles,' he says.

He doesn't know about Trump, Mike Pence, Kelly Anne Conway, Sean Spicer, Fox News, Putin, Assad or Kim Jong Il. He doesn't know about the all-rounder, Brexit or Marine Le Pen.

'Marine Le Pen,' I say, aware that since the thing with the dog, my voice has not come right.

'Run, Daddy,' he says.

And so we run. Him on the gravel, me, still protecting my knees, on the grass, down towards where his blankie will always be trapped in the backflow caused by water falling.

DI STARRENBURG

By the Roots

'I've come about the aloes,' Ada says. The door frame dwarfs her. Her sweater dwarfs her. Her hair is spun by a silkworm. 'Those awful things along your fenceline.'

Alex is surprised to learn that her memory has not exaggerated this woman's hostility. Since they moved back to the house, Ada's face has watched from windows and shifted behind curtains.

'They're dangerous,' Ada says. 'They're just hideous.'

A hint of urine blows in with the breeze.

Madeline needs a bath and is crying for crackers. She sinks down and thrashes like a fish on the floorboards. Alex used to do the same as a toddler, eyes rolled back, lips blue. Her mother never panicked because she'd done it too, right here on the matai—held her breath and woken with her nose against the borer lines. Her daughter's outburst reminds Alex of her mother, as do the cabinets stuffed with lotions, the coats at the back of the wardrobe, and the Tupperware dangling with webs and weevils that she scrubbed and re-stacked in the pantry, the way they were when she was a child. Even the little Cavendish in her belly reminds her of her mother. It is obstinate. It kicks her in the ribcage.

'So you're the daughter,' Ada says, and scans Alex from her stiff jaw to the slippers on her feet. There is a cataract in one of Ada's irises, wet and milky. 'Fancy I'm the one who gets to see you grown.'

Alex's mother used to hate this woman. Her grandmother even more so. That she stands here on Cavendish land outliving them both is an amusing sort of justice.

'Anyway,' Ada says, her wrinkled lips pulling down, 'the aloes will hurt someone, a child riding past on a bike. I wrote to the council.'

'It's just like the car,' Jarrod says that night, over spaghetti. 'We were fined two hundred dollars for parking on our own verge.'

'That may not have been Ada.'

'On a dead-end street?' His chair scrapes across the floorboards. 'In the middle of the night? We can't afford her shit. We can't afford our *power bill*.'

I quit my job for you, is where this conversation leads. The baby rolls inside her. She'll vomit if they talk about money again. She wants to stack pre-mushed vegetables in the grocery cart without guilt about her desire to move to Havelock North. She wants to talk about how this house has saved them. This house is saving them. Within these walls of faded birds and berries they can live rent free. But Jarrod needs a job, so despite the autonomy her mother has given them by dying, he insists they need to talk about money.

'Isn't it enough,' he says, 'that we're paying for her to live?' Jarrod stares at Alex. She once traced her thumb over his sleeping forehead and marvelled at his eyebrows, one higher than the other—cynical while unconscious. 'You know the stats,' he says. 'Our grandparents paid sixty cents of tax for one dollar of services back. We pay *two dollars* per dollar of services. We're *paying* for them. *Her generation has not paid its own way*.'

Alex reaches for the plates and bumps the calla lilies. Orange dust scatters across her forearm.

'And now,' he says, 'it's the fucking aloes.'

Her mother's aloes. She rinses the pollen and yellow stains her skin. 'They're just plants,' she says.

'Exactly, and they're ours. I'm not cutting them for *her*.'

Jarrod seeks refuge in the study of Old Man Cavendish. It has stayed the same since he passed years ago—heavy furniture, dim light, books on aviation and arthritis. The extra room is a luxury they couldn't afford in Auckland. Alex should see it as a good thing that he skulks away in there. He'll soon become accustomed to living with more than a cupboard-sized bedroom and a metre of pebbles for a garden.

She never expected that the study, once out of bounds, would be hers. Her mother and grandmother refused to enter it, believing that men like Old Man Cavendish were allowed to keep secrets if they tucked them in a corner and let their wives pretend they had nothing to hide. Alex never imagined the past would be handed to her in this way. Any secrets, discoverable or not, are now hers. Even the coffee stains on the mantle are hers.

A foot, or an elbow, presses against her bladder and Alex holds herself as if the baby might slip out. She snaps a hardened bud from the rose bush, deadheading while Madeline stirs mud on the grass. Through the thinning hedge she sees Ada on her patio, weeding pots of purple leaves that haven't changed in years. Ada puts a palm to her forehead to block the sun, then waves for Alex to come over.

As a child she would have hidden, or run, but Alex's actions are no longer swayed by the prejudice she grew up with, and so she wriggles through the hedge. Madeline skips at her ankles, frosted with mud.

'I'm glad I spotted you,' Ada says. 'I need a bulky sort of person to help me move my sofa.' She dusts soiled hands across a gardening apron and walks indoors.

The comment is meant to be insulting, and Alex has to remind herself that her youth gives her flexibility; it allows her to more easily dodge the insults of the small-minded. She tells Madeline to stay on the porch and pluck snails from the flowerpots.

Half the light dissolves behind Ada's doorway. A stained-glass window makes patterns on the carpet and Alex remembers being no older than five while Frances sat beneath these colours. Frances was a teenager then, and therefore enchanted, and the blue and yellow light crawled over her legs while she bled from the nose. It could have been dry air, or allergies, but Alex saw red caked to Frances's upper lip and pictured the back of Ada's hand snapping a bone.

'A mouse got underneath it.' Ada points a finger at the brocade couch. 'I can't get to the mess.'

With her back straight and knees bent, Alex shifts the couch by a foot. A skin of dust coats the carpet, slivers of fingernail, and mouse droppings thick as maggots.

Ada hands Alex a dustpan and brush. 'I'd never get back up,' she says.

Alex's cervix tugs as she lowers. She reaches forwards with the brush and breathes through her mouth to mask the smell while dust and droppings roll in lumps onto the shovel.

Over the years she uncovered many childhood mysteries, such as whether a piercing would deem her unemployable, and was she too helpless to live on her own or would leaving her mother empower her, and did her father ever wish to meet her? Coming home brought one last unanswered question to the fore: Ada.

'You're more helpful than Irene,' Ada says. She is backlit by the window light, but her eyes can be seen despite the shadows. This is the way Ada used to stare, with this expression of hatred. Alex rewinds—coming in she was curious, even benevolent, but now she feels the way she used to as a child, like prey.

'How well did you know your grandfather?'

The question is confusing, and unnecessarily hostile. Ada shuffles forwards and on reflex Alex stumbles back, mouse poo scattering. She lands on her tailbone and the baby squirms.

'You've made even more of a mess,' Ada says.

'Alex, are you in there?' The sound of Jarrod's voice brings a measure of relief. She fast-walks, her spine and hip joints protesting, into the light. On the porch there is dirt everywhere. The flower pots have been rummaged through and dug up, and Madeline has muddy fingers. Mud on her chin and in her hair.

Jarrod stands at the foot of the stairs with a letter peeled open in his hands.

'What have you done, girl?' Ada steps from the door frame, her look of horror directed at Madeline.

'The aloes,' Jarrod growls, 'are not encroaching on the footpath by more than an inch. Now we have to remove them unnecessarily and pay.'

'How dare she?' Ada turns to Alex. 'Are you a true Cavendish, then? Have you taught your child no manners?'

The fetus lashes out.

'What's your problem?' Jarrod spits.

Madeline scurries across the porch, squealing about a bee. She ducks inside the door frame in her mud-caked shoes. Blue and amber light from the stained-glass window twists up her shoulders and over her head.

'Stop, girl.' Ada's hand stretches towards Madeline's collar. Alex lunges to pull her daughter back but she knocks Ada's shoulder and Ada tips towards the flower pots with a gasping *oh!* An exhale. A pot clatters and more dirt spills on the porch, and Ada hovers, suspended at the edge of the steps. Jarrod goes to grab her but the patio is slick with green growth and his feet fumble. Ada's back lands on a step, her head cracks, her body overturns. She slumps to the concrete.

'Christ, Alex!'

The arm of Ada's cardigan is splayed—unfurled like a wing.

'Christ, Alex!'

Blood makes ribbons down the back of Ada's neck and her skirt is hiked up past her thighs. They are spotted with flaking sores.

'Mummy, it was a beeee!' Madeline shrieks.

Alex stumbles down the porch steps.

Crouched next to Ada, Jarrod gingerly fingers her neck. 'Oh my God,' he says and pulls out his phone. Then: 'What the fuck are you doing?'

Alex is fumbling with pieces of broken terracotta, stuffing flowers and dirt back into smashed containers. She gives up, begins to sit, and stops herself. The steps are smeared with blood and potting mix.

At 6:15, Ada is pronounced dead. Alex was retrieving Madeline, she tells the police. Madeline was helping to weed the flower pots.

'Do you weed flowers?' The man bends down to ask. The dirt on Madeline is mixed with dribble and tears. 'I find snails.' She sniffs and Alex holds her.

'Quite close with your neighbour, were you?' he says.

'I've known her all my life.'

'That porch is overdue for a waterblast. It was an accident waiting to happen.' He places a hand on her shoulder and squeezes lightly. 'I'm so sorry for your loss.'

At night she lies awake and sees her hand meet Ada's cardigan, feels the bones beneath. The body thumps, blood pools. The push was rash, meant to separate Ada from Madeline, but it had not caused death, she tells herself. Neither had the damp wood and moss, the concrete stairs. It is almost poetic how such damage can be caused by so small a thing: Ada's life ended because she fell. Alex has seen terminal disease disfigure a body, and as she bunches her sheets beneath her chin she decides she would prefer a fast blow to the head.

Jarrod is avoiding her—his presence has been reduced to scrunched tissues and lozenge wrappers deposited around the house, distant throat clearing or the flushing of the toilet. He has not mentioned Ada's fall since the ambulance doors clicked shut on her corpse. The two occasions she has spoken to him—both with his face beneath a pillow—he has used the house against her. His allergies have flared from mildew, from the way water streams down the insides of the windows in the morning. The latest piece of him that she has stripped away, by moving here, is his health.

With Madeline down for a nap, Alex taps on the door of her grandfather's study. The windows are open despite the chilly air, and the lace curtains flap and fold. Jarrod is at the desk with a wheat-pack over his shoulders, still wearing pyjama pants. A glass of Scotch is balanced on the arm of Old Man Cavendish's chair.

'Trying to induce a fever?' Placation is not Alex's goal—his silence draws more blood than his bite, so she wants to bait him. He does not meet her eyes, just stares at her belly until Alex feels the need to shield her fetus.

'You told me I would find a job,' he says, eyes hooded. 'I haven't.'

'I saw something at Ada's house.'

Jarrod flinches. The name is cursed.

'When I was there with Madeline.' She'd seen blood on the concrete, the light of a sconce reading lamp left on in the living room, and Ada's armchair dipped in the middle by her ghost. She'd seen a security camera—a black box aimed at the front porch.

'*Alex.*' His look is one of disgust. 'You're *killing* me.' He leaves the room and a piece of her skin goes with him; she is raw, vulnerable.

For the rest of the day Madeline hides in the closets and pushes her soft toys down the laundry shoot. She is oblivious to her father's mood and climbs on him on the sofa like a bird settling on a tiger. Jarrod eats by himself and then he is gone—the back door has clicked shut and the car has left the driveway.

The house groans in the dark and Alex cannot lie awake in it. She leaves the glugging walls, the fluid curtains, and Madeline asleep with her hair sprung like wild grass. Outside, the air is cold and wet lawn slips beneath her shoes. Ada's porch is still lit by the living-room sconce as Alex pulls herself up onto the verandah railing, hugs a wooden beam and perches there, metres above the flowerbeds. She breathes as if in labour.

The camera is attached by a magnetised ball that easily comes free of its mounting. Her guilt fits neatly in her palm. She studies it. The compartment at the back contains batteries only. The footage will be digitised on an app somewhere, in a scramble of zeros and ones, with newly filmed data of Alexandra Cavendish for whoever is watching.

Television light flickers across the road. A vehicle rumbles and the sound grows louder. Headlights illuminate the cul-de-sac.

Alex hugs the pole and shuts her eyes, pretending to disappear.

The car slows and idles in front of Ada's house. It will be a neighbour or a do-gooder. People in small towns feel a need to engage that frustrates Alex. In Auckland, every car would speed past.

She peaks around the pole.

Jarrod. His head dips to peer at her through the passenger window. She cannot tell, through the darkness, what his expression says, but when the car rolls on around the hedge and the engine dies, she knows. This is *her* guilt, his footsteps tell her. If she wishes to bury herself deeper, he will continue to walk away.

Alex cannot settle. It has been two days, and Frances must be due to arrive. Attempts to remove the traces of a crime involve committing new ones. The roots tangle and spread. Over dregs of her fourth cup of coffee, Alex decides she will use Old Man Cavendish's crowbar to force a lock to snap.

Little Cavendish is made of stronger stuff than Madeline, who panics at her mother's grunts and squeals when woodchips fly from the beam and Ada's back door swings open.

'Look,' she says to Madeline, 'but don't touch.'

Madeline trots in and out of rooms where life lingers after death like warmth in a slice of toast, a damp towel and deflated suds in the plughole. Beside the computer are Watercare bills, a radiology report, a bank statement. Alex wiggles the mouse and the computer screen lights up. She types into the search engine. Ada's email is not recognised on the security company website, but *Frances McKinnon* is remembered as a login name. Frances. Alex recoils from the desk. Frances has the footage. She reshuffles the mail pile and speed-walks down the hallway, the urge to leave descending like a ghost.

Madeline is sitting before an open drawer in Ada's bedroom, with strings of beads, photos, scarves and costume earrings scattered like the aftermath of a dress-ups game.

'*Madeline!*' Alex drops to her knees and stuffs objects back into the drawer. 'I said don't touch!'

'A baby!' Her chubby fingers grip a photo of Ada with baby Frances in her arms. It is the sixties. Bright dresses and bulbous hair. Ada's young eyes glance at the camera as if her name has been called.

'Nana,' Madeline says.

That word triggers an unexpected shock of pain. 'You didn't know your nana.' *Your nana had no desire to know you.* The thought is feeble, unwarranted, and heady with the narcotics of self-pity.

A loud knock judders the frame of the house.

'Someone's at the door, Mummy!'

'Shhhh.' Madeline wriggles when Alex wraps a palm over her mouth and pulls her into the wardrobe. With a finger to her lips, urging her daughter's silence, Alex sits on Ada's shoes. Their heads and shoulders are draped with Ada's musty clothing. Alex waits for the knocker to leave, then escapes down the hall and out the back door. The fetus steals her blood supply. It brings black fuzz to her vision.

Alex scrubs rough skin off her heels until the waterline clouds with scum. She is twisted and tangled like her hair in the water, like weeds. A car engine outside brings her to the edge of the bathtub, to see over the windowsill. Beyond the hedge, someone is moving and shutting doors. Alex wraps herself in a dressing gown.

Jarrod sits cross-legged on the study floor. Open files of old papers are spread in a sea around him. He is the image of his daughter, fishing through Ada's jewellery drawer, except at his age the look is repulsive.

'Your grandfather,' he says, 'owned more than one property.' He rattles a paper. 'At least two. And no mortgage. Yet his grandchildren are so full of debt they're *shitting it* while paying for the super of the baby boomers who were handed a free education and a goldmine in the dirt under their feet. And they can't even boast that they fought in the war.' A fleck of spit lands on his lip. 'How's *that* for intergenerational inequity?'

Alex turns to the window. She can see Frances. Frances has grey hair now, in tight poodle curls. She paces between her car and the porch. Has she viewed the footage? Will she call the police about the busted back door? These thoughts drive Alex to drink a glass of Scotch in the dark kitchen, swirl naked up the stairs, her engorged belly pale in the moonlight, and mount Jarrod on the chair of Old Man Cavendish. Madeline dances with her in the hallway, eyes wide with confusion and surprise at this exhilarating version of her mother. But Alex hears nothing from Frances, and for three days no police arrive to arrest her.

When Jarrod's presence becomes only slightly more discernable than the other ghosts in the house, Alex buttons a plastic coat over Madeline and takes her to the park despite the rain, and to the dairy for ice-cream. The local paper lists obituaries on the back page. Ada's body is at Morton Funerals until Thursday's service, and Alex cannot quite understand her need to walk kilometres to the funeral home, but she feels it is something akin to wallowing in a breakup or pressing an injury to make the pain flare.

She slips through the entrance, spilling rain. Soft music plays and the walls are lined with glass orbs of ashes.

'Is the lady dead, Mama?' A lump of soggy cracker is stuck to Madeline's cheek. She points at the receptionist. '*Is that* lady dead?'

Alex speaks Ada's name and is ushered into a room occupied by a coffin.

'Take your time,' the receptionist says. 'There are tissues just here.'

Alex plucks a rose petal from a basket and slides it back and forth between her fingers. Madeline is on her toes, chin over the rim of the casket. Alex can see folded hands. White spun hair. She steps closer.

Ada's face is askew as if it has been moulded from putty, and collapsed. Makeup coats the pallor. Was this what her mother looked like, only weeks ago? Alex did not know; she had not come until afterwards and felt the weight of her in a small, plywood box.

She had not driven to Havelock North when she heard her mother was sick. She was pregnant, she had a small child. She refused to be manipulated. Perhaps it was selfish to stay away but she remembers the vigil-like way her mother nursed her grandmother until her death, and the expectation for Alex to do the same was suffocating. The last time she laid eyes on Irene Cavendish was eighteen years ago.

Was her skin this yellow when she lay in her casket? Her eyelids, the same almond shape as Alex's, unnaturally painted with blue? Perhaps her features were distorted from illness, her face puffed into a moon.

Constellations glitter in the foreground.

She lets her petal go and it drops in the coffin. A siren is sounding, and Madeline says something but her voice is muffled.

Alex stirs from the sort of sleep she craves. Her dreams are a blur of voices above her head, and she wants to bury herself into the pillow but the pillow is a prickle of carpet on her cheek.

'You fell,' says a shadow with sour breath. 'We're worried about the baby.'

She inches up to sitting on the floor of the funeral home, ignoring the dizziness. Madeline is with the receptionist, her face red and splotchy, and a woman in scrubs presses a glass of water into Alex's hand.

'How are you feeling?' she says.

Alex lies back down on the carpet.

She dozes on the drive to the hospital, with Madeline at her side. Nurses wheel them together, mother and daughter under a blanket on a stretcher. The baby's heart rate echoes in hoofbeats through the CTG monitor, and Alex stares at the hospital curtain listening to her grandmother's voice.

Have you seen the way that woman dresses, the late-night visits from male and female alike? Hussy! she hears. *That poor child.*

Their hatred for Ada was never explained. Like Grandfather's disappearances to the study, or elsewhere, but never to the kitchen and very rarely to Alex. Sometimes she saw him in the hallway in the evenings, with a pipe and in a robe. He got away with never being around, as the Cavendish family got away with their hatred of Ada, the witch next door.

Once Alex spied over the fence while Ada watered the garden and a strange urge overcame her. She took her apple core and biffed it. It hit the grass not far from Ada's feet and rolled. Ada lifted her hose towards Alex and droplets rained down.

It was not until later, when she could be stifled no longer and left, that she gained perspective enough to distrust the things she'd learned as a child. To see hatred for what it was. Perhaps Alex could explain herself to Frances—she was a pregnant woman, a bereaved pregnant woman. She'd reacted out of fear, out of protectiveness. Perhaps she and Frances could rip the secrets and conflicts out by the roots?

'Another ambulance.' Jarrod stands at the foot of the stretcher. 'You could have called if you needed a ride.' His puffer jacket is wet and Madeline clings to his leg. Facial hair has grown in tufts that spread like desert grass from his neck to his cheekbones. She doesn't ask where he's been.

On the ride home, red and green lights shine in streaks across the tarseal and Madeline draws in the condensation on the windows.

'I've been in contact with Ryan Adgrave,' he says. They still haven't found a replacement for me and they're desperate. I'm heading back tomorrow.'

The indicator marks the seconds. Four clicks.

'They need me.'

Jarrod is indispensable.

Click-five, click-six, click-seven.

He glances at her but she turns her attention to Madeline. 'You okay, baby?' Alex wiggles her fingers until her daughter's slippery palm grips her thumb.

It's not until they reach the driveway that Alex looks at Jarrod. 'You've been busy,' is all she says, because the aloes are cut back from the Cavendish fenceline to half the size, maimed and glistening.

'I've come about your mother.' Alex, Madeline and the Cavendish Seedling hover on Ada's doorstep. 'I've come to talk, if that's okay?' All plant pots are cleared and the porch has been waterblasted. Frances is dark and silvery and looks like Ada, only generationally closer and therefore more tolerant. More forgiving, perhaps.

Inside, much of Ada has been stripped back for sale. The sofa is clean, the carpet bare. Frances makes tea and they sip out of mugs that have, Alex hopes, been scrubbed like everything else. Madeline scales the back of the couch, imbued with her mother's nervous energy.

'You looked out for her,' Alex begins. 'You were a good daughter.'

'I haven't been here as much as I would've liked.'

'You …' She'd practised this at home, weeding the secrets, but that does not make the moment any easier. If Frances has not seen the footage by now, she will at some point. It would be best to tell her first. To explain. 'You even put security cameras in.'

'Pardon?'

'On the porch.'

'Oh, yes.' Frances smiles, remembering. 'She once thought someone was stealing her mail so we had a camera installed. No one ever changed the batteries but I doubt she knew it needed them.'

The little Cavendish flips. 'The batteries are dead?' She feels confused, light-headed.

'Yes, but the camera gave her peace of mind. It might have even warded off a few potential criminals.' She laughs lightly.

The carpet spins. Madeline slips and knees Alex in the back but she barely feels it.

'Look,' Frances says. 'I'm glad you're here, because there's something I've been meaning to come and talk about. I've wanted to see you but … it's awkward.'

'You don't need to feel awkward.' Alex dives into cordiality. She wants to be the good neighbour, to hug and laugh and have Frances leave and to never see her again.

'I found some documents. I've discussed them with my lawyer and, well, your grandfather appears to have had an indiscretion.'

'My—what?'

'With my mother,' Frances says.

Old Man Cavendish … and Ada. Memories clunk into place. The name-calling and shaming. They knew. My mother and grandmother knew about an affair. 'Well,' Alex says. 'That actually explains some things.'

Frances looks relieved, as if she hadn't expected Alex to take this well. She sits on the edge of the sofa. 'So, as it turns out, I'm a Cavendish.'

Alex opens her mouth to form words that don't come.

'I don't know,' Frances says. 'Am I supposed to miss my father now, or hate him?'

'My grandfather?' Alex hardly knew him, but she now feels for sure that he was a devious, selfish bastard. How dare he? How dare her grandmother stay, and live next door, and keep his secrets? Perhaps Jarrod had rubbed off on her because her loathing for Old Man Cavendish feels far-reaching, linked to his generation. To all they got away with and never answered for.

'So the thing is,' Frances says, 'this is the important part.' She hands Alex a letter. 'This letter says he bought her this house. She had nothing and he looked after her. I guess it wasn't something he felt he could do—leave your grandmother, that is.'

Alex unfolds the letter. It's written in the spidery script of another era.

'This is the crux,' Frances says. 'She had to pay back half to his estate if she ever sold. And I'm selling, so half is yours. The value of the house has gone up somewhat since the sixties. We're expecting, I think, somewhere in the high six-hundreds.'

Alex has been on the verge of tears since she knocked on the door, but now Frances is the one who cries. She inches closer and wraps her arms around Alex. 'It's so strange,' she says. 'He was right there and I never knew him. Oh! Your mother. I heard.' Frances looks Alex in the eyes. 'I'm so sorry for your loss.'

She lets Frances give her the comfort; lets Frances view her as someone who deserves it. She runs her palm over the letter. She can imagine Jarrod tearing through the silence with a line that upholds the peace long enough to secure his money. We'll miss Ada, she was special, he'd say. The baby is still, but a feeling unravels from the tangle in her chest and flutters towards her throat. A new shoot, sprouting.

'Me too,' she says. 'I'm sorry for your loss too.'

ALAN RODDICK

What Happened

My true love's mother's best friend
    Norah College

came once only, uninvited,
    to see my father.

She greeted him as 'George', as if
    they'd met before.

They sat out on the lawn to talk,
    out of earshot.

He poured two whiskies
    and got his pipe going,

she smoked her pocketful
    of roll-your-owns,

and my mother and I
    speculated.

Afterwards he told me
    'That woman used words

your mother doesn't know.'
    She wondered which ones.

Norah said to me, 'I thought
    he talked good sense,'

though what they discussed
 remained a mystery.

But when I left town
 for my chosen career

and one month later
 my true love called me

to say that same week
 she meant to be married,

I had to see, through telephone tears,
 just what happened.

LINDSAY RABBITT

Delivery

Shy boy
in the
doorway

handing
over his
light touch

JASMINE TAYLOR

Lines to Meaning

A viewing of Gordon Walters' The Poet (1947), *pencil and oil on canvas*

Approach from left as attention's caught
Narrowing the gaze from macroscope
Eyes resolve humanoid, anthromorph
Curving lines into seated figure
Lean in; the title, The Poet.

Jointless knee supports elbow's repose,
Handless arm allows faceless head rest,
An oval housing oval becomes
Mouthless face; and wafting line rises
To left; is that line a poem?

      A poem is made of gathered lines
      This Poet is made of curving lines
      A poet is a curver of lines
      And the lines are made of gathered words
      Words that lead to a notion inside
      Directing meaning outward toward
                       the viewer

And this viewer has conjured a meaning.
And did this artist intend that meaning?
Perhaps they're two parallel lines

RICHARD REEVE

Dog with its Head out a Window

Love it, love it, love it, love it, love it.
I take a sample from the atmosphere.
The summer wind blows leftovers I covet,
my tongue a sop to suck up seasoned air.

The fields fly past, cows monitor the road
for veering yapping, moo and drop their horns.
I eat a breath of beetles, laugh out loud
to be the dog and tell off their newborns.

Good just to be, my head out the window,
yelling at nothing till they shut me down.
On, on it goes, the hare on the windrow,
gulls pecking dust in a field out of town.

Bark at the moon, apparent at midday,
growl at the goat in the bitten-back hedge.
Take up a front seat, my whiskers muddy,
to yelp at the dangler on a distant ledge.

DAVID EGGLETON

Caselberg Trust International Poetry Prize 2018 Judge's Report

In poetry, there are no compulsory prescriptions. What matters is the vitality of the writing. Poetry is the most pragmatic of disciplines: what works, works. Reading the more than 150 entries for the 2018 Caselberg Poetry Prize, I felt like a bloodhound truffling for the scent, the spoor, of the finest poem, unearthing it from a rich tilth of possibilities.

There were poems about identity, political and personal; and a poem about Anzac Day; a poem about MGM movie moguls; a poem about 'having trouble with words'. There were poems about Aleppo, Amsterdam, the Catlins, the Gare du Nord. One poem discussed banning Philip Pullman for swearing; another, the sensation of being embraced by Mother India; two poems debated the feminist gaze versus the male gaze. There was a poem about Peter Olds' jacket by an admirer.

One motif met with over and over in these poems was birdlife: in particular, native birds of all kinds, soaring and swooping and fluttering through light and shade as if emblematic of the pulse of life itself—from fantails above Mount Maunganui to a falcon 'kiting old Hawkdun grey'. Another motif was a matter of tone: the deployment of a sidelong laconic manner that seemed expressive of a particularly New Zealand way of writing poetically about experiences.

Sincerity was a constant: sincere emotion, sincere assertions, sincere belief in the power of the poem to tell the truth. Well, perhaps. But a poem must also be full of verve, agile in its language, artful in its crafting. The best poetry blindsides you with the unexpected, so that you feel you must immediately revisit it, dwell on it, absorb it: you are the music while the music lasts, wrote T.S. Eliot.

In the end I selected six poems that are all very impressive pieces of work. 'Astonish me,' the impresario Sergei Diaghilev challenged his dancers in the Ballets Russes; these poems do that. Other poems had their moments, but these finalists have a satisfying sense of completeness in every aspect.

I was taken by the alertness of perception displayed in 'A Country Airing', and the way its compressed descriptions were all neatly dovetailed into place. It is a poem that, in the words of John Updike, 'gives the mundane its beautiful due'. 'The Castle' is a poem where domestic incidentals—a telescoped autobiography—are combined into a zigzagging metronomic unity, with a heartening homeward turn at the end, using the compass of the twenty-six letters of the alphabet. Each line is cleverly buckled into place by its alphabetically ordered beginning letter. The poem 'Memorial', naming and remembering, is a kind of allegory, reminding me of Robert Frost's claim that 'the land was ours before we were the land's'. Here, the old colonial order or repressiveness is still being wrestled with, while the lushness of regenerating native vegetation and wildlife, even in suburbia, asserts the return of the true order of things. The poem 'Oh! Kee-o Kee-o'—a sonically charged title—has a heartbeat-like pulse animating its nervy language. With its empathy for the natural world framed by the exigencies of the modern world, it is part epiphany, part psychodrama—and will jolt you with its electric flash of tension, like sparks arcing.

There's a certain magisterial resonance conveyed by the poem title 'Full Measure' that is borne out by the poem itself. It is a graveyard poem that asserts, with Shakespeare, that 'ripeness is all'. Ruminative, both sardonic and affectionate, it is a poem in which the poet writes with a eulogising immediacy of unquiet graves and of the entanglements of generations. If the poem has a saturnine cast, it is also lapidary, as if chiselled in communal stone.

The poem 'you can't be here' has a quicksilver radiance; it's like some febrile emanation of human consciousness itself. I applaud the wit and vividness of its dream-like scenario. In its zaniness and absurdity, it's a kind of distillation of our current cultural condition, making it up as we go along in a just-in-time manner. A poem, in order to be true to itself, must find its own form and confidently express that form all the way down. This poem does that. It obeys an internal logic that is organic, harmonious and wonderfully expressed. Evanescent, spun out of thin air, it generates its own force-field; it lifts you up—and puts you down in a different place.

The winning entry is 'you can't be here' by **Derek Schulz**, and the runner-up is 'Full Measure' by **Tony Beyer**. The four highly commended entries are 'Oh! Kee-o Kee-o' and 'Memorial', both by **Janet Newman**; 'The Castle' by **Sarah Scott** and 'A Country Airing' by **Ruth Arnison**. All these poems are published on the Caselberg Trust's website.

DEREK SCHULZ

you can't be here

They dropped Gem on the road where it was continuing to bucket down, so I ducked out with the lobby umbrella and scooped her up from where no one else was looking. She was feathery and light as a korowai, and had just finished dripping so there was nothing left inside, but I took her up to my room as if she was still here then held and held her, until I'd called her back. It took about a week, and another before she began to move; then cooked up her favorite invalid stew, kūmara and pūhā. The pūhā was just where she said it would be, in the lobby planter, growing behind the dahlias. You wring it out like your underwear, under the bathroom tap. Screw and screw and screw it until the bitterness flows right out, then boil it up with the kūmara, skins and all. Mash & feed, mash & feed, mash & feed, that had been her Māori regime and every day she seemed to glow a little lighter under it, until suddenly her eyes flared open. I asked her what she could see. –Is that really you? she said, as if she dare not make up her mind. Yet then ... –Nothing, she decided. There's nothing in here, grey clouds of it. –Okay, I said. I need you to hold your breath. –Okay what? –You heard. Pretend you're under water, just like in the old days. See how long you can stay down. Just do it! She took one last gulp and did exactly as she was told, which was a real worry. She'd never done that before, though half an hour later she'd forgotten who she wasn't, and gotten right back to herself. –Now tell me what you see. –Blue, she said. Everything's turning blue. Should I have started breathing by now? It had worked. –You can't be here, I said. They only take the train wrecks. When the M finds out they'll send me away. –But I'm dark, she said. I've gone totally dark. It's won me over. Her men had begun collecting on the far side of the bed. They wore blue-beards on their T's, over purple Jagger jumpsuits, but she couldn't see them any more so I star-war'd them away with my sky-walker scarf. –Tripe, I said. You're going home. Mitzy's on her way. Mitz was her step-sister, the ugly one, and arrived in a Mirage around 8.30. She barrelled through those front doors as if she'd only just heard the news, then drove it up the stairs to the front door, up here on the fourth floor, before busting right into the room. I could see she still blamed me for everything but never said a word, just bundled her into the car, then roared back down the hall. That's Mitz for you. You wouldn't think you could drive a Mirage around those hotel landing corners, but she made it look effortless. Then took the lift back down. Such a queer place this. No air to speak of and everywhere you look has just been made up.

TONY BEYER

Full Measure

they buried him with his mother's people
whom he hadn't seen since childhood
the best part of a century ago
but not having to shift to make room for him
they were as welcoming as ever

the wind that deposited grit
in the pitted parts of their gravestones
sang to him as well
of the bones of ancestors interred
in the soil of more distant islands

to his left a cousin of his grandfather's
reposed under a snippet of Paul
as intellectual as religion got
among farmers horse fanciers
and founders of the nation's railways

sequestered in another yard
the absent progenitor whose name
was hyphenated with a slur of surnames
paid for eternity in exile
the price of his spiritual curiosity

back in the approved dynastic plot
in dust at his feet three nieces lay
beheaded beneath a jack-knifed trailer
on the coast road driving their way
to an abruptly disbanded reunion

their names intertwined with flowers
on their monument are the names of flowers
recalling that descent too ceases with death
along with succession and breath
the prerequisites of inheritance

antidote to those who go about
with the suspicion that those in the cemetery
enjoyed the best of this land
its simpler rustic pleasures
its unquestioned entitlements

CALL FOR ENTRIES

CHARLES BRASCH YOUNG WRITERS' ESSAY COMPETITION

An essay competition for writers aged 16–21.
Entries open on 1 December 2018 and close on 31 March 2019.
The prize for the winning essay is $500, a one-year subscription to *Landfall* and publication of the winning essay in *Landfall*.
See the Otago University Press website for more details: https://bit.ly/2xDJqwP

LANDFALL

Landfall Review Online
www.landfallreview.com

Reviews posted since April 2018
(reviewer's name in brackets)

April 2018
Sleeps Standing Moetū, Witi Ihihmaera with Hemi Kelly (Simone Oettli)
Low Life, Michael Botur (Bret Dukes)
Fresh Ink, multiple authors (Bret Dukes)
Aukati, Michalia Arathimos (Sue Orr)
Rāwāhi, Briar Wood (Ben Brown)
My Wide White Bed, Trish Harris (Ben Brown)
Ternion, Vaughan Rapatahana (Ben Brown)
Iceland, Dominic Hoey (Louise Wallace)
The Fuse Box, eds Emily Perkins & Chris Price (Courtney Sina Meredith)

May 2018
Sodden Downstream, Brannavan Gnanalingham (Kiran Dass)
Beneath Pale Water, Thalia Henry (Craig Cliff)
The Necessary Angel, C.K. Stead (Kate Duignan)
Body, Remember, Wes Lee (Diane Brown)
Anchor Stone, Tony Beyer (Diane Brown)
The Trials of Minnie Dean: A verse biography, Karen Zelas (Diane Brown)
Poetry and Exile: Letters from New Zealand 1938–1948 by Karl Wolfskehl, ed/trans Nelson Wattie (Norman Franke)
You Do Not Travel in China at the Full Moon, ed Barbara Frances (Alison Wong)
Old Asian, New Asian, K. Emma Ng (Alison Wong)

June 2018
Driving to Treblinka: A long search for a lost father, Diana Wichtel (Helen Watson White)
The Cage, Lloyd Jones (Chris Else)
The Expatriates, Martin Edmond (Nelson Wattie)
Polly Plum: A firm and earnest woman's advocate, Jenny Coleman (Jane Westaway)
Cleansing the Colony: Transporting Convicts from N.Z. to Van Diemen's Land, Kristyn Harman (Lucy Sussex)
Instant Messages, Laura Solomon (Carolyn McCurdie)
Taking Wainui, Laura Solomon (Carolyn McCurdie)
Brain Graft, Laura Solomon (Carolyn McCurdie)

July 2018
The Man Who Would Not See, Rajorshi Chakraborti (James McNaughton)
Whisper of a Crow's Wing, Majella Cullinane (Siobhan Harvey)
Threading Between, Dorothy Howie (Siobhan Harvey)
Pasture and Flock: New and selected poems, Anna Jackson (Siobhan Harvey)
Disobedient Teaching: Surviving and Creating Change in Education, Welby Ings (Bernard Beckett)
Dear Oliver: Uncovering a Pākehā history, Peter Wells (Barbara Else)
South D Poet Lorikeet, Jenny Powell (Vaughan Rapatahana)
Walking to Jutland Street, Michael Steven (Vaughan Rapatahana)
The Light and Dark in our Stuff, Mere Taito (Vaughan Rapatahana)
he's so MASC, Chris Tse (Vaughan Rapatahana)
Marlborough Man, Alan Carter (Jenny Lawn)

August 2018
Tuai: A traveller in two worlds, Alison Jones & Kuni Kaa Jenkins (Briar Wood)
Dawn Raids, Oscar Kightley (Simon Cunliffe)
Mazarine, Charlotte Grimshaw (Linda Burgess)
False River, Paula Morris (Rajorshi Chakraborti)
Rotoroa, Amy Head (Denis Harold)
American Retrospective: Poems 1961–2016, Eleanor Rimoldi (Murray Edmond)
Foreign Native, Lisa Samuels (Murray Edmond)

September 2018
Floating Islanders: Pasifika theatre in Aotearoa, Lisa Warrington & David O'Donnell (David Geary)
Aspiring Daybook: The diary of Elsie Winslow, Annabel Wilson (Mary Cresswell)
Are Friends Electric? Helen Heath (Mary Cresswell)
Winter Eyes, Harry Ricketts (Mary Cresswell)
Work & Play, Owen Bullock (Mary Cresswell)
Semi, Owen Bullock (Mary Cresswell)
Gordon Walters: New vision, eds Lucy Hammonds, Laurence Simmons & Julia Waite (Peter Shand)
Performing Dramaturgy, Fiona Graham (Emma Willis)
The Facts, Therese Lloyd (Michael Steven)
Punctuation, Rogelia Guedea with trans Roger Hickin (Michael Steven)
Tinderbox, Megan Dunn (Rebecca Styles)

The Landfall Review

Savage Punishment
by Mark Broatch

This Mortal Boy by Fiona Kidman (Vintage, Penguin Random House, 2018), 304pp, $38

Memory tells me there used to be a plaque in central Auckland, in a spot now occupied by a glassy bank building, for the last public execution in New Zealand. Turns out my memory was wrong; it wasn't the last—that was Walter Bolton, in 1957—but the first. Wiremu Kīngi Maketū, the son of a Ngāpuhi chief, was perhaps 18 when he was hanged for murder on that spot in 1842. He was also the first Māori person to be publicly executed. The plaque is not obvious these days—perhaps it's been quietly removed and junked, like so much inconvenient history. But Maketū is in the history books, along with the other 80-odd people (and five military personnel) put to death by the state for their crimes.

Because too few read history books, we know almost nothing about these poor souls, apart from Minnie Dean, the only woman executed, and Bolton, whose guilt was doubted in a TV programme a few years ago. But now, the second-last to die, Northern Irish immigrant Albert Laurence Black, has had his case posthumously reassessed courtesy of an ambitious novel by Fiona Kidman. Albert Black, aka Paddy, was hanged in Mt Eden jail two years before Bolton, on 5 December 1955, for the murder by knife of Alan Jacques, aka Johnny McBride. When Black—the book effectively argues that he suffered an egregious failure of justice—stayed in Auckland, it was at a boarding house just up the road from Maketū's scaffold. Perhaps there was a plaque back then, though probably not. We're thankfully not proud of such savage punishment.

Kidman, who has fashioned novels from the lives of other notable Kiwis such as aviatrix Jean Batten, has performed in *This Mortal Boy* a terrific feat of imagination. Each of Black's jurors, his lawyer, his former landlady, his lover, his prison superintendent, his parents—all make an appearance. They look, sound, act singularly. Places are distinct, from hotels where people drink or deliberate, to rooms and houses where people party or contemplate the horror of Black's misfortune. All characters are invented or their names and circumstances have been changed, though a few real people show up, such as Attorney-General Jack Marshall, who's painted as a hardliner, and later stripclub owner Rainton Hastie. Sometimes it's harder to tell where the fictional line lies. A killer called Horton, who was imprisoned because the death penalty was not in force, sidles up to Black in his last days issuing slurs and slights like Wormtongue. In real life a man called Horton was imprisoned for a terrible murder, but reports suggest he changed his life.

I have one problem with the novel, but it is an unavoidably pesky one: Kidman has clearly done so much research, knows so much about the man Black and his misfortunes, that the early pages are flattened by detail, much of which may have been better held till later or left on the cutting room floor. Passages read as overworked. Characters explain things.

Let me offer a few examples.

'Albert's mother had told him not to go over there, it was too far away from Gay Street that ran off Sandy Row where they lived.' 'She had been surprised that Bert was a man who sang the way he did, because he came from such a strait-laced family who had little music in their hearts, but he had been in a choir at school in England and it seemed like melody just stuck to him.' (Though 'stuck to him' is enviable.) 'Paddy wondered if Buchanan thought he wouldn't know what the Mazengarb Report is. But he does, because he lived on the doorstep of that government-commissioned document which claimed youthful lawlessness and immoral behaviour was sweeping the country.' With all due respect, I suspect a young, popular Irishman would be busy creating moral panics rather than heeding them.

Inserting era-identifying events into historical fiction without clunk can be tricky even for the best writers. One of the jury wonders if Princess Margaret will marry that divorced chap Peter Townsend. Others look out of a hotel to a half-completed harbour bridge, trams, a bustling railway station. Fair enough. But would the chaps in the jury (no women) really talk about a rugby test from weeks ago? 'Several of the men had been at the game, and they relived the nail-biting anxiety of the final minutes when the whole series was on a knife edge. The relief of it, not getting licked by the Australians … Ken thinks the boy on the stand might have heard their voices raised in rejoicing from his prison cell just along the road from the park.' We meet the jury all at once. Some readers may prefer this; others may, as when being thrown into a vast crowd of inlaws, feel overwhelmed and wish to encounter just a few at a time.

Clichés are employed. 'In the night his spine tingled with terror.' '… his heart swells with longing.' Things are repeated. That's me, Paddy thinks, twice within a few pages. The superintendent, we're told twice, has the awful job of preparing the condemned man for the gallows. Johnny McBride, it's pointed out more than once, was a Mickey Spillane character. A witness recalls telling Paddy to stop making threats otherwise he'll 'get hanged' and a few pages later 'get hung' (it's possible she might say both, even if the accepted use is explained later).

Yet sometimes a fact is apposite. That it will cost Paddy, a literal 10-pound pom, twelve times that to get back to the UK. That a condemned man is weighed every day, to get the right length of rope, but also so he doesn't know what day it's going to happen. That people once danced delightedly at the Orange Hall and later at the Māori Community Centre, but that Māori families might stand outside the jail, 'their wailing and sobbing rising in torrents of sound'. That moral repression was the norm; and that repression is a whack-a-mole endeavour: while condoms were banned for the young, unless you knew the right fruiterer or pie cart, there's incredible carnality, people shagging all over, despite the risks.

And sometimes a description perfectly brings somewhere to life:

> He sees it in the swimming light of a winter evening, a long room with a bar counter along one side, flanked by six high stools where you can sit and drink Bushells coffee, dark liquid poured from a square bottle, topped up with boiling water from the Zip, eat a steak or a hamburger, or a frankfurter, and across from there, cubicles that fit six at a squeeze, three on either side of a Formica-topped table lit by low-hanging lanterns. The room leads through a latticed wall adorned with flowering pot plants to the jukebox.

Paddy is overwhelmed by homesickness, particularly once the judicial machine starts to rumble, and a sense of doom pervades the latter part of the book. 'Still, he couldn't stop listening to the bird sounding its melancholic haunting notes, as if it were coming for him.'

The lawyers get the best lines, I reckon, in that elevated, carefully passionate language intended to inject doubt. 'All around you, in this courtroom, you are surrounded by the beauty and vitality of youth, as well as its vanities and arrogance. The young occupy an uncertain universe. Mistakes can be made in the heat of the moment.'

And what about these: 'It had slipped out, little black eels of words making their own truth.' 'The memory of his mouth on her nipple stirred her even now, flooding her like the urge for sex.' 'Dawn was breaking, the clouds parting, sullen bonfires of light falling between them.' Or the rough vigour of Paddy's encounter with an older woman, which delightfully surprises. More please.

The fact is, once I'd got further into the book, I wanted to tell the author: forget the details, we trust you. This novel could have lost its first fifty pages and would have only gained. Plunge us, in medias res, and let us find the shore ourselves.

The actual execution is detailed, dispassionate but unmistakeably condemnatory. Few will fail to be overwhelmed by revulsion for the sheer brutishness of the death penalty.

I would have loved to learn in the acknowledgements whether one or two people, such as Paddy's last lover, were real and, if so, whether they are still alive. If she's entirely made up, well, the author has done that difficult thing of creating wonder beyond a book's pages. Overenthusiastic fact-finding aside, *This Mortal Boy* is to be praised for its sustained storytelling and moral vision. Albert Black is likely to be remembered in a new, more favourable light. It is almost certain that among the 80-odd executions yet unexamined more terrible injustices are to be discovered.

Challenging Complacency
by Tom Brooking

Strangers Arrive: Emigrés and the arts in New Zealand, 1930–1980 by Leonard Bell (Auckland University Press, 2017), 310pp, $75

One of my favourite New Zealand history books is Leonard Bell's *Colonial Constructs: European images of Maori 1840–1914*, published in 1992, so I came to his latest book with high expectations. Generally those expectations were not disappointed—this is an erudite, well-written and beautifully produced book. Congratulations to Sam Elworthy and Auckland University Press for the stunningly reproduced black and white photographs and etchings and the richly coloured paintings. The cover is also striking, featuring a Frank Hofmann photo on the front and Douglas MacDiarmid's painting *Figures at Night* on the back.

The book takes the form of four chapters—on photography, painting, writing and architecture—bookended by pithy essays (one at the front and two by way of a conclusion and epilogue). In a book of this type the chapters tend to be lists of artists, but they are very interesting lists.

Within them Bell makes a powerful case for art and cultural historians to pay more attention to this influential and highly talented group of people, many of them Jewish; in particular painter and polymath Frederick Ost (Czechoslovakian); photographers Frank Hofmann (Czechoslovakian), Irene Koppel (German), Maja Blumenfeld (German), Franz Barta and Richard Sharell (both Austrian); painters and sometime informed art critics and commentators Patrick Hayman (English), Jan Michels (Dutch) and Margot Philips (German); potter Mirek Smíšek (Czechoslovakian); sculptor Frank Szirmay (Hungarian); art commentator Gerda Eichbaum (later Bell, German); architects Imi Porsolt (who also designed chairs, Czechoslovakian), Gerhard Rosenberg (German), Vladimir Čačala (Czechoslovakian), Henry Kulka (Czechoslovakian) and Helmut Einhorn (German); furniture designer Ernst Plischke (Austrian); and lastly bookseller Robert Goodman (Austrian), who introduced so many Aucklanders of my generation to the delights of Tintin, Asterix and C.S. Lewis. Between them, these creative people, influenced by the Bauhaus in particular, helped modernise New Zealand painting and architecture, challenged complacency, and opposed anti-intellectualism. They thereby greatly enriched the country, and especially Pākehā culture, in the process.

Bell adds three long-forgotten New Zealand-born painters who 'escaped' in the other direction to Europe because they too felt like 'strangers' (Flüchtlinge in German). Douglas MacDiarmid moved to Paris, leaving behind much challenging work, while James Boswell based himself in London and produced a wide range of paintings, but remained neglected in his homeland. So too did Douglas Glass, even though he won some recognition in both England and France where he became a close friend of Frances Hodgkins and an acquaintance of Charles Brasch.

Bell concludes by focusing on Brasch, who managed to return from England and feel more comfortable so far away from his central European Jewish ancestral home; essentially because he at least gained peace and security in New Zealand. The epilogue ponders the future artistic impact of the increasing number of refugees in recent times. Bell hopes that their creative responses to the difficulties of living in an alien culture and often experiencing 'occupational degradation' will produce just as enriching a response as that made by those fleeing the horrors of Nazism in the 1930s.

Bell argues that most of these émigrés felt displaced in New Zealand, but they surely would have done so anywhere in late 1930s Britain outside the cosmopolitan centres of London, Dublin and Edinburgh. Xenophobia is not uncommon in the midst of a major global war. Here I became concerned with Bell's central premise that New Zealand was a smug, provincial backwater whose citizens had little interest in either the arts or the 'life of the mind'. Surely this characterisation is becoming rather clichéd and is an unnecessary cultural cringe, given that many exciting things were happening in New Zealand in the late 1930s. Life was simply not that dull at this point in our history, even if disillusioned World War I veterans persuaded the likes of John Mulgan that they had returned to an ungrateful country.

Political reforms created a fully developed welfare state and the first Labour government made huge efforts to promote high culture. The Workers' Educational Association, assisted by Carnegie Foundation support for libraries from 1938, broadened New Zealanders' reading habits. James Shelley, a formidable champion of high culture, overhauled broadcasting and modelled both the YA and YC radio stations on the BBC. The National Film Unit was established in 1941, partly to provide coverage of New Zealand's war efforts so that our role in the global conflict was recorded for posterity, unlike in World War I, where naïve local audiences watched official British propaganda masquerading as news. The National Orchestra emerged immediately after the war in 1946. Prime Minister Peter Fraser also wanted national ballet and opera companies but lost office before he could realise those dreams.

These state-sponsored and community-supported cultural efforts were reinforced by important educational reforms as Fraser consulted with a wide variety of overseas experts and brought in the high-flying educationalist (not a supermarket chain operator) Clarence

Beeby to overhaul the curriculum. Indeed, the educational programme offered by H.C.D. Somerset at Oxford District High was in advance of anything previously seen and, arguably, of anything attempted since. These advances built on a long tradition of having the highest literacy levels on the globe.

There was also plenty going on in writing and painting under the perhaps unlikely stimulus of the Depression as artists took advantage of the spare time induced by higher levels of unemployment. One only needs to think of The Group in Christchurch, especially Rita Angus, Evelyn Page and Bill Sutton (in addition to Colin McCahon and Toss Woollaston, whom Bell does talk about). Then there were Robin Hyde, John A. Lee, John Mulgan, Denis Glover, Allen Curnow, A.R.D. Fairburn and Frank Sargeson, not to mention the underrated Jean Devanny, Ursula Bethell, Elsie Locke and Jane Mander before them. Even photography was advancing, with the likes of Gary Blackman and John Pascoe going on to make significant contributions in the 1950s. Architecture may have been something of a backwater but young New Zealand architects were champing at the bit and ready to engage with modernity—a desire that produced its horrors as well as triumphs. Modernity was not always best.

Drama and choral music were strong within local communities, as even the acerbic high-brow critic Charles Bayertz had acknowledged much earlier in the 1890s. By the 1930s cities like Dunedin, thanks in part to their Jewish benefactors, but also because of the Scots' love of education, were quite cultured spaces. Burns was still well known, both the Art Society and Art School thrived, and the city boasted a large and successful choir as well as a mighty organ to accompany it. My own mother was a gifted pianist and organist who introduced me to the joys of classical music and played with members of the National Orchestra when they visited our Dutch neighbours (surely a group whose cultural contribution deserves more scholarly scrutiny).

Bell's Eurocentric viewpoint is useful in balancing out the older Anglo-centric viewpoint but, despite the sympathy of some émigrés for the plight of Māori, he also overlooks exciting developments in the Māori world. Apirana Ngata may have locked Māori into rather traditional ways of making art down to the 1950s, but then a new generation of Māori artists emerged to push those traditions in exciting new directions. Ngata's carving school in Rotorua also revitalised that and thereby greatly enhanced many new marae. Ngata and Te Rangi Hīroa meanwhile saved much mythology, history and story and many waiata for future generations.

I discovered during some recent research of my own that there were several worthwhile histories written in the 1930s in addition to J.C. Beaglehole's *The Exploration of the Pacific*. W.P. Morrell's general history of New Zealand (1935) is very good and much more comprehensive than Beaglehole's sprightly but light general history. And then there was Te Rangi Hīroa's Vikings of the Sunrise. The nationalist literary establishment and its views as articulated by Robert Chapman in this very periodical in 1953 greatly exaggerated how dire and dull writing and arts of all kinds were in the period before those same masculinist nationalists became pre-eminent.

New Zealand became more hedonistic in the 1950s as returning soldiers tried to forget the horrors of war by seeking normalcy and suburban ordinariness while the country became more prosperous and governments more conservative. Bell needed to talk about such shifts rather than presenting the long 1930s–1980 period as a homogenous whole. Even the 1950s was not nearly as dull as Bell and many other historians try to make out, despite the fierce denials of artists who developed their craft during that decade.

There can be no doubting that the émigrés from Nazism made a special contribution and added flavour and spice to New Zealand photography, painting, writing and design. As both Kate Camp and Catherine Chidgey commented at a recent public event during a celebration of Janet Frame in Oamaru, like modern-day European artists, the émigrés brought a concern with thinking about deep matters rather than being satisfied with simply describing their doings. Even so, the émigrés were adding to something that was more substantive than is generally acknowledged. Certainly their efforts constitute an important and too often neglected tributary, but the mainstream was (and is) rather more interesting and vibrant than its detractors suggest.

Despite this misgiving, this is a fascinating book of considerable appeal to anyone interested in the development of high culture in New Zealand. And it is a timely reminder of the dangers of any retreat into a 'laager' mentality, as it highlights the significant cultural contribution that refugees can make to any country.

Continued from page 88
Notes
upega: net
fa`alupega: naming of chiefly titles of a village
va: space
malu: protection, women's tattoo
tautai: fisherman
tupuaga: ancestors
taupou: daughter of a matai/chief, virgin
aiuli: to make much of
siva: dance
va`a: canoe
Pulotu: residence of the gods/afterlife/
   underworld

Transgressive Reappraisals
by Janet Charman

Telling the Real Story: Genre and New Zealand literature by Erin Mercer (Victoria University Press, 2017), 386pp, $40

A signal contribution to critical writing in Aotearoa New Zealand, Erin Mercer's *Telling the Real Story* is a refreshingly wide-ranging survey of the critical reception of realist vs. genre novels in this country.

Mercer is fully affirming of genre fiction and convincingly demonstrates that the supposed barriers between realist and genre modes are in fact significantly porous. She also shows that realist narratives have historically been attributed an authenticity and legitimacy conceived of as normatively masculine; with genre fiction all too often critically marginalised as feminine-other. Mercer itemises how such relegated genre work, especially the melodrama narratives she affirms (in for example, Jean Devanny's *The Butcher's Shop* and Sylvia Ashton-Warner's *Spinster*) sucessfully express transgressive ideas with which patriarchy was, and still is, out of sympathy.

Mercer's approach is not limited to one critical perspective, however. For example, addressing Laurence Fearnley's *The Hut Builder*, Mercer is alert to metafictional, environmental and historical approaches when she describes Fearnley's work as 'a realist novel that purports to accurately reflect local realities and an intertextual novel that uses past modes of representation to comment on the present' (Mercer, 276). She shows that the novel's material and secular view of the Southern Alps celebrates their wild sublime without recourse to the ominously judgemental Christian orthodoxies found in the poetics of Ursula Bethell, James K. Baxter and Allen Curnow. But she also notes that Fearnley's protagonist remains happily oblivious to any myths from indigenous occupancy, so evading *unsettling* references to colonisation.

Mercer herself is not immune to such cultural blindspots—but are any of us? For example, in her analysis of *The Hut Builder* she does not address the hostility towards women writers which Fearnley's hero, Boden Black, encountered in *A Book of New Zealand Verse*. This is the Caxton volume edited by Allen Curnow (1945): its contents motivate Boden, an untutored small-town butcher, to become a respected practitioner of the poetic arts. In fact, in an implicit denial of Curnow's opinion that poetry by women was inferior (which he reinforces in his Penguin introduction), Fearnley's protagonist is entranced at discovering Ursula Bethell's 'By Burke's Pass' in the anthology. He is made to pointedly recuperate the very features of Bethell's poetics that Curnow singles out for disparagement: 'recondite words, illplaced or perverse phrasing; others are overborne by descriptive phrases and mannerisms' (Curnow, 44). Boden, by contrast, comes to a full accommodation with Bethell's style, noting: 'Words that had filled me with annoyance now aroused my curiosity' (Fearnley, 86). In her long quotation from this section of Fearnley's text, Erin Mercer allies herself with this reframing (278).

Curnow's introductions to his Caxton and Penguin anthologies of the postwar period were expressly calculated to stifle the 'flowery' register of the romantic feminine. In his dismissal of work he considered inauthentic, Curnow relegated all but a handful of the women poets who were his peers to nonentity status. This process allowed him to claim sole legitimacy for the male as a neutral-universal voice he idealised as 'genuine', an authenticity that Fearnley's novel also attributes to Boden Black.

But strangely, Mercer's analysis does not register Fearnley's subtextual acknowledgment of the trauma of those women whom Curnow and his age cohort effectively excluded from both literature and public life during the postwar decades, before the feminist resurgence of the 1970s. This silencing is felt in Fearnley's symbolic treatment of the character who is Boden's adoptive mother. She spends her life sunk in a depression so unremitting that the child Boden, in a desperate attempt to escape contamination from her enveloping cloud of sadness, attaches himself to, and then moves in with, the family across the road. Unable to deal with her child's self-imposed exile, his adoptive mother fills the empty hours by doing large jigsaw puzzles while continuing to produce roast dinners for her husband.

Her unhappiness is attributed to her repeated miscarriages, losses compounded by the deeper trauma of the World War II naval drowning of her twin adult sons. But the extinguishment of feminine [pro]creative agency seen in this character can be read as Laurence Fearnley's symbolic response to what John Newton has characterised (in misleadingly naturalistic terms) as the 'hard frost' (Newton, 2017) that the masculinists of Curnow's era prescribed for any creativity found to be identifiably feminine. John Newton takes this phrase from Charles Brasch's approving summation of Curnow's critique of local poetics as having 'killed off weeds' (Newton, 19). But actually a 'weed' is simply a plant somebody decides is in the wrong place.

Laurence Fearnley's use of a first-person male voice for her artistically revered protagonist therefore recognises that in Boden's era, to be heroically successful a poet must be male: with his success symbolically contingent on insulation from the utter abjection of his m/Other.

There are undoubtedly those who would prefer not to hear any more analysis of the inadequacies of Allen Curnow's critical perspectives on women's writing. Perhaps it is this anticipated hostility that explains both Mercer's and Fearnley's reticence to deconstruct Curnow's phallocentric assumptions about the literary canon of

Aotearoa New Zealand. But hesitancy to address this topic seems akin to avoiding the #Me Too movement. Recognising who gets denied the opportunity to participate in our cultural productions and why is the only way to begin to remedy such exclusions and produce more and better work—for equal pay.

Yet the calculated mildness of tone in Erin Mercer's critiques of Aotearoa New Zealand literature doesn't make her work complicit with dominant narratives. Despite some tactical withdrawals, Mercer's analysis, even more than John Newton's recent and intriguing critical evaluation of the same period, actively avoids the temptation to offer simplistic venerations of canonically celebrated texts. Mercer's acute examination of some of our most dismissively assessed fiction resists critical complacency and argues that such work deserves as much notice as that which is currently well recognised and loved.

Mercer repeatedly draws attention to the ways in which both marginalised and mainstream Aotearoa New Zealand novelists resist and exploit genre boundaries. From her diaspora analyses I particularly enjoyed her illumination of the realist grounding of the fantastical in Robin Hyde's *Wednesday's Children*. She also considers why the gothic elements of Keri Hulme's *The Bone People* were initially overlooked, and goes on to evaluate the ambiguities of this novel's treatment of child sexual abuse. Mercer also notes the subversiveness with which the long-disparaged genre features of

'sensation' novels have been deployed by Eleanor Catton in *The Luminaries*, so as to affirm and enrich the non-realist elements of the local literary tradition. Mercer's canny analysis of Elizabeth Knox's *Daylight* makes it possible to infer that the realist 'Kiwi' elements of Knox's vampire novel are seen to slyly re-emerge in Jemaine Clement and Taika Waititi's tragicomic, locally set vampire movie *What We Do in the Shadows*.

However I must dissent from Mercer's analysis of David Ballantyne's novel *Sydney Bridge Upside Down*. Mercer maintains that the unwarranted obscurity of this text is the result of its uncertain genre: 'In a literary culture that was still defined largely by the realist mode, Ballantyne's move from the mimetic art of social critique to *something that defies generic categorization* was bound to be fraught [my emphasis]' (Mercer, 150). This supposed difficulty of classification actually reflects a cultural denial of sexual trangressivity. In fact *Sydney Bridge Upside Down* is readily classifiable as a trauma narrative, examining the horrific effects of child sexual abuse. It has uncannily close parallels with the short story *Vandals* by the Nobel Prizewinning Canadian author Alice Munro.[1] Indeed, with their similarly monstrous imagery of animal torture, and the only ostensible incomprehensibility of their victimised protagonists' behaviour, it is tempting to speculate that there could be a direct link between these two texts. The 1968 first edition of Ballantyne's novel was produced by an Australian publisher, so

Munro may well have encountered *Sydney Bridge Upside Down* during her 1980 writing residency in Queensland.

The peculiar nonsensicality of Ballantyne's title hides in plain sight what is actually the key to its transgressive thematic concerns. A horse owned by Sam Phelps, the perpetrator of child sexual abuse towards the now adult first-person narrator Harry Baird, is named 'Sydney Bridge Upside Down' because it has a sway back. The cause of this deformity is ascribed by Phelps (in conversation with yet another boy he has begun to sexually groom) as the result of 'too many heavyweights on him when he was a youngster' (Ballantyne, 189). For the attuned reader there comes here the metaphorical realisation that while still 'a youngster', Harry has equally been made to carry the 'heavyweights'—not only of the adult Sam Phelps' sexual violations of his immature body, but also of his parents' and community's denial of the sexual crimes to which he has been subjected. This is what produces the metaphorically 'sway back' psychological deformity in Harry, which across the course of the narrative escalates to stunt all his relationships, both then and in his adult life.

Erin Mercer, despite her detailed reading of *Sydney Bridge Upside Down*, is silent with regard to the sexual abuse which is in fact its central concern.[2] It's a troubling omission, since Ballantyne's novel, which is alert to patriarchal culture's longstanding failure to acknowledge and prevent the sexual exploitation of children, predates *The Bone People*—whose child sexual trauma narrative Mercer does carefully examine.

An equal concern is the fact that Mercer's impressive registry of the influence of John Mulgan's novel *Man Alone* on the realist narratives of generations of male Aotearoa New Zealand writers makes no reference to its homoerotic subtext. Rather, Mercer focuses on Alex Calder's re-estimation of this iconic work as owing a romantic genre debt to the 'western' (Mercer, 93). But attributing to Mulgan's protagonist a 'John Wayne or Clint Eastwood' lone 'cowboy' persona does not acknowledge Mulgan's subtextual critique of the colonising oppression of the 'Indians' (qua tangata whenua). In fact in *Man Alone* racism towards the indigenous is treated as inextricable from European misogyny and homophobia. This critique is carried by Mulgan's hero, Johnson. Therefore it is wrong to suggest, as Mercer and Calder do, that Mulgan privileges 'attention to his protagonist's physical presence rather than his psychological depths' (Mercer, severally, 94).

The specific example offered as representative of Johnson's 'flat characterization' is Mulgan's description of the hero's making a roll-your-own cigarette as a merely 'bodily action' (Calder in Mercer, 94). But in fact this is an exemplar of the 'making of a fag' trope that is used emblematically throughout the novel to construct and celebrate Johnson's homoerotic sensibility (Charman, 2010, 36–38). In the instance Mercer quotes, Johnson is awarding himself a Fag in recognition of his violent defence of Scott—his lover— from a police attack. Continuing critical silence on the subversive resistance of *Man Alone* to institutional homophobia, as brutally meted out in Mulgan's era by The Law, is evidence of patriarchal hegemony's still actively repressive effect on Aotearoa New Zealand literature.

That in some significant respects Erin Mercer's otherwise credible and perceptive analysis follows convention in her under-reading of *The Hut Builder*, *Sydney Bridge Upside Down* and *Man Alone* illustrates how critical dismissals and genre segregation of the many texts she analyses here have substantially limited our recognition of the depths and diversity of local literature. As Mercer herself points out in her introduction, there are many 'other' texts worthy of the close analysis she applies. In particular I would love to read her take on the deceptively polite gothic-horror novels of Tina Shaw.

The arguments made in *Telling the Real Story* should produce greater critical receptivity to transgressive reappraisals of local fiction that is currently under-read or marginalised.

Works cited
Ballantyne, David (1968), *Sydney Bridge Upside Down*, Introduction by Kate De Goldi (Melbourne: Text Publishing, 2010)
Charman, Janet, *Smoking: The homoerotic subtext of Man Alone, a matrixial reading* (Dunedin: Genrebooks, 2010: www.genrebooks.co.nz)
Curnow, Allen, *A Book of New Zealand Verse*, (Christchurch: The Caxton Press, 1951)
Curnow, Allen, *The Penguin Book of New Zealand Verse* (Harmondsworth, Middlesex: Penguin Books, 1960)
Fearnley, Lawrence, *The Hut Builder* (Auckland: Penguin Books, 2010)
Newton, John, *Hard Frost: Structures of feeling in New Zealand literature 1908–1945* (Wellington: Victoria University Press, 2017)

Notes
1 Corinne Bigot, '"Locking the Door": Self-deception, silence and survival in Alice Munro's "Vandals"', in *Trauma Narratives and Herstory* (Palgrave Macmillan, 2013).
2 Mercer offers a detailed analysis of the climactic scene in *Sydney Bridge*, which I interpret very differently as follows:

The climax of the child protagonist Harry Baird's psychological deformation comes when he watches his cousin Caroline having sex with her boyfriend Buster. In this scene Harry secretly observes as this couple enact a mutual sexual exchange in which consent is dynamically structured moment by moment in interactive facial and body language. But then comes a penetrative act (initiated by his cousin) which Harry's torturer Sam Phelps has formerly inflicted on him by means of coercion and restraint. As he watches, Harry's identification is not with Buster, but with Caroline, as he subjectively/objectively references her expression of jouissance as antithetical to his own rapes. The last sentences of this scene refer to Harry's experience of being forced into the very sway-back position which he sees Caroline now joyfully adopt of her own volition. A position whose anguished associations for Harry are symbolically reified in the ongoing exploitation and suffering of the horse. Drawing on his memories of Phelps' sexual assaults, Harry attempts here, and fails, to make sense of Caroline's perspective: 'Hit by hammers, stabbed. How could she let such a huge thing go into her? No wonder she laughed at mine, no wonder she gave it a baby name. I was a baby. He was a man. I could do press-ups all day long, all week long, and never be like him' (Ballantyne, 259). These last remarks reference Buster, but relate to Phelps and in them Harry recognises that as 'a youngster' he can no more transform himself so as to take on his abuser (as Buster could)—than he can take on Caroline. Harry's horrified acceptance at this moment that as a child he is powerless without adult support is the trauma that precipitates his running away to the anonymity of the city, so heralding the novel's ominous denouement.

Like an Operatic Quartet
by Gail Pittaway

Gabriel's Bay by Catherine Roberston (Black Swan/Penguin Random House, 2018), 428pp, $38

Any reader drawn to this first edition's cover image of summer catalogue pastels, sand dunes and deckchair, or by Catherine Robertson's happy association with the romance genre, is bound for a deeper, richer read than expected. *Gabriel's Bay* wisely refrains from the picturesque or breaking-waves scenario so popular in beach art. Robertson's town is an anywhere-and-everywhere coastal New Zealand settlement: ribbon development along the stretch of bay with supermarket, two pubs (one closed), a petrol station, doctor's surgery and pop-up café. The nearest town is Hampton, 'just over the hill' by way of a windy and precipitous country road.

So far, so conventional. However, the rotating point-of-view narrative—bookended by that of King, the resident black Labrador—offers a wider sense of perspective than the simpler focus of escapist fiction, and in its shifting viewpoints we find the background detail, motives, decisions—flawed and sensible—which make for the generation of more than one narrative focus. Like an operatic quartet, *Gabriel's Bay* offers a complex multilinear approach, where each character has her or his own preoccupations and unique inner dialogue, with idiomatic voice. This dialogue, both inner and articulated, gives the novel its breadth combined with moments of sheer humour.

Even the most flawed and hapless characters possess a credible motive; there is no evil in Gabriel's Bay, only ignorance and deprivation.

At the heart of the novel are the everyday concerns of small towns anywhere—shrinking population, poor infrastructure, isolation, urban drift and an ageing leadership, most strongly identified in the character of Doctor Love. Now well into his seventies, Love's compassion and patience have nourished his clients for decades, but Mac, his receptionist, who knows the secrets of most of the patients and has few good words to say about them, is concerned about succession. Not only is the doctor's personality irreplaceable; he will also be impossible to replace, given the difficulties in attracting a new professional to their remote back water. Unlike many summer holiday beach hamlets, Gabriel's Bay does not seem to have the accordion-like capacity to expand and contract seasonally. It is what it is; take it or leave it. And many seem to have left it.

Into this sedate settlement comes Kerry Macfarlane, escaping a jilted bride and disappointed families back in the United Kingdom. A series of short-term jobs has brought him across the world to accept a role as caregiver and housekeeper for the Bartons, Meredith and Jonty. He has been employed under the misapprehension that Kerry is a woman's name and is put on a trial to prove his domestic capabilities. Given a living and brief reprieve from travelling, Kerry finds himself in a complicated household dominated by a man who refuses to turn away from the wall, let alone recognise the many decades of love and sacrifice of his intelligent and sensitive wife.

Through Skype and phone calls, Kerry resumes contact with his Irish mother, the source of his first name, and more remote father, back in England, as he gradually builds networks in this community which, though superficially friendly, has its own complex depths for him to discover. His mother works as a strong off-stage voice, giving him advice down the phone lines from her years of nursing to guide him to break though the dome of inertia that sits over his employers' household and the emotional stranglehold held by its invalid owner.

Kerry is ready for a change and finds himself drawn into the larger community, through his own initiatives and also at the request of others who warm to his energy and sincerity. There's Bernard whose decades-long unrequited love for Meredith has impeded any joy in his marriage to Patricia. Jock and Gene entertain readers and characters alike as the older 'blokes' whose café offers their own hunting and fishing produce and is the 'Rover's Return' of the novel—the fulcrum of community and a fine eatery.

The younger generation are also well depicted, especially the young men—Sam, Barrett (Brownie), Deano and Tubs—whose incoherent amity is threatened by the impending breakup of their gang, as Sam prepares to leave the bay for an apprenticeship in the city. Meanwhile Barrett's future has been derailed by his father's chronic illness. Each of these relatively minor characters generates unexpected events that braid through and push along the many lines of story.

Then there's Sydney, a woman with an equally androgynous name as counterpart to Kerry, but she is not entirely willing to play the female lead in any romance novel. Most touchingly there's nine-year-old Madison, whose yuppie parents, Rick and Olivia, can't keep their money or their marriage tight and whose rows and absenteeism are cause for concern. Madison's love and loyalty for her selfish parents are heartbreakingly expressed in the chapters written from her perspective. Robertson's management of the tensions arising from the clashes between breadline poverty and excessive overspending among people from a range of social classes is comprehensive and admirable.

The author's style is crisp and sharp, and her dialogues possess a brisk freshness that contributes considerably to the charm of the novel. Her characters are not small-town simpletons, and this is not a simple story. It shows the catalytic impact of a stranger upon a small town, and the far-reaching consequences of well-meaning enthusiasm. Despite her well-established reputation as a writer of lighter fiction, with six previous novels and short story collections, Robertson swerves across the white line onto a bigger causeway with *Gabriel's Bay*.

Star Trek, Samoa and Seduction
by Gina Cole

Freelove by Sia Figiel (Little Island Press, 2018), 182pp, $30

Playful workings of language bookend and encapsulate Sia Figiel's Oceanic tale of star-crossed love between seventeen-year-old Inosia Alofafua Afatasi (Sia) and her teacher, Ioage Viliamu. Sia's name, Alofafua, translates as 'Freelove' in Samoan, and questions surrounding this play on words are a central motif in the book. Figiel's prose is lyrical and lushly layered, poetic and grounded in Samoan culture. *You have turned me into a woman who seeks nourishment in coconuts that fall at midnight. Husking them with my teeth. Drinking their forbidden juice.* One lovely page consists entirely of script resembling Samoan tatau (tattoo) in an innovative, uniquely Samoan portrayal of climax.

Book One (of two), entitled 'Inosia Alofafua Afatasi', covers the period from October, in Sia's last year of high school, to January the following year when she leaves Samoa and travels to America to study. It begins with a list of English vocabulary, a list of Samoan–English vocabulary, Sia's final school report from Mr Viliamu, and a list of the top twenty best songs of 1985: from Madonna's 'Like a Virgin' to Whitney Houston's 'Saving All My Love for You'. These metafictional texts read almost like poetry and serve to introduce Sia's interior world, her place at the top of the class in science, and Mr Viliamu's glowing report of her as 'a rare gem' and 'intuitive and mature beyond her years'. This unconventional beginning to the novel immediately unsettles the narrative and alerts the reader to several themes running throughout the book—love and sex, illicit relationships, tradition versus Western notions of science, religion, the media, female roles and power.

The next few pages begin with Captain James T. Kirk's opening monologue from the 1960s television series Star Trek: 'Space: the final frontier …' Star Trek is Sia's own personal mythos threading through the novel. She is a Star Trek fanatic—remembers every episode of season one, measuring her life against the values and lessons she has taken from those stories. She is also fascinated with words, science, and the place of black women in science, such as Lt Uhura in Star Trek. Throughout the book there are many such intertextual references to pop culture: science fiction in particular. This literary device is one of my favourite features of the book.

Figiel situates the influence of 1980s television soap opera and Western pop culture within the context of Sia's life in Nu`uolemanusā Village, and the fact that there are only three TVs in the village. They belong to the pastor, to Queeniveere's family, and to the village sa`o or head chief. She cannot watch TV at the house of the sa`o, as it is sacred, and no one goes there except to drop off food. She cannot watch TV at the pastor's house—'it was rather awkward to watch people show intimate affection on Fantasy Island or The Love Boat or Dallas while Tāmā Esimoto prepared his sermon …'. This leaves only one house where Sia, and other members of the village, are able to watch TV: the house of Queeniveere or 'Q'. This is clearly a reference to the mischievous 'Q' character in Star Trek (yes—I am also a Star Trek fanatic). We are only briefly introduced to Sia's friends: Q the 'tomboy' who has romantic feelings for Sia, and Cha the fa`afafine. I wanted to hear more about Q and Cha, but apart from another brief appearance at the end of Book One there is no further development of these characters.

The suspense begins when Sia tells us she is about to embark on a similar voyage to Star Trek's—a 'life changing journey' into a 'strange new world' where the 'rules of civilization as we know it' are abandoned. She is talking about the forbidden world of incest, 'the final frontier'. We are told that Sia loves someone she calls 'Night', who is her brother and her lover and also her teacher, Ioage Viliamu. We are introduced to Mr Viliamu when Sia's mother, who is sewing shirts and puletasi for White Sunday, sends Sia on an errand to Apia to buy white threads. Sia accepts Mr Viliamu's offer of a lift to Apia; Mr Viliamu insists she sits in the front with him. So begins Sia's seduction, which takes place over the space of that day. Mr Viliamu starts by deliberately exposing himself, then 'accidentally' brushing up against her, and insisting that she call him by his first name, Ioage. This disturbing scene is both shocking and perplexing for Sia and the reader. Confused by the sensations she is feeling and the power differential in age and position between her and someone she has previously looked up to and admired as a teacher, Sia tries to make sense of what is happening to her by engaging her formidable scientific mind.

Mr Viliamu, now referred to as Ioage, drops Sia off in Apia, and while walking through town she tries to process her feelings about the incidents in the truck within the framework of *Star Trek* stories—'like the supernova explosion' in the 'All our Yesterdays' episode. We realise that perhaps Mr Viliamu has been seducing Sia for the whole of her education, introducing her to Western scientific and mathematic theories and notions so that they run parallel to traditional Samoan concepts of the universe. Sia's feelings about her teacher flip from academic admiration and respect, to shock at the sexual approach, and finally to romantic thrall and desire as she decides to meet Ioage and accept the five-hour ride back home with him.

It dawns on Sia that she may now be in a 'relationship' with Ioage. The problem she immediately realises is that he is the pastor's oldest son, which 'technically made him my brother' and makes their relationship forbidden in fa`asamoa, Samoan custom. Their relationship is taboo because although they are not related by blood, they are nevertheless regarded as `āiga or kin. Their relationship is also forbidden because Ioage is her teacher.

The remainder of Book One traces the sexual and emotional relationship between Sia and Ioage over the course of the truck ride and diversionary stops they make on the way back to the village, and the emotional and physical consequences for Sia. As the day progresses, Sia's respect for her teacher turns into 'something else', a burgeoning sexual awakening culminating in her deflowering at the lake. In exploring the connection between Sia and Ioage, Figiel employs the concept of the vā, which Albert Wendt has described as 'the space between, the between-ness, not empty space that separates, but space that relates, that holds separate entities and things together in the Unity-that-is-All, the space that is context, giving meaning to things'.[1] Sia is constantly trying to assess the nature of the vā between her and Ioage and the forces ranging around them, through discussions and thoughts about colonisation, Western notions of romance, science, love, sex, indigeneity, Samoan cosmology, legend, tatau, and ideas of Samoan masculinity. Often the only way Sia is able to deal with her struggle to come to terms with the forbidden nature of her sexual awakening is to mediate the experience through the lives of TV characters such as the wealthy women in *Dallas* and the femmes fatales of *Star Trek*. By the end of Book One Sia is preparing to travel to America to begin her university studies, and she is also pregnant with Ioage's child.

Book Two, entitled 'Ao ma le Po, Day and Night', comprises a series of love letters between Day (Sia) and Night (Ioage). These letters contain poetic musings on Samoan legend and custom and the impossible union between Day and Night. We learn that Sia becomes a student at UCLA, studying to be a physicist while pregnant with a daughter called Sa, who she refers to as Spacegirl. Figiel investigates the issue of solo motherhood versus career as Sia struggles with the decision about whether or not to give up the baby so she can go on to study thermonuclear fusion. Thus, having surpassed Ioage intellectually, Sia is cast into the conundrum of having to choose between being a mother or a pioneering scientist.

I really enjoyed reading Sia Figiel's *Freelove*. It is wonderful to read long fiction by a Pasifika woman that has a strong, intelligent, female, Pasifika protagonist, and deals so insightfully with themes of identity, colonisation and so much more. Most of all, as a woman of Indigenous Pasifika descent myself, and a writer of fiction, I feel proud to be in the company of another Pasifika woman writer who is clearly a sister *Star Trek* nerd.

1   Albert Refiti, 'Making Spaces: Polynesian architecture in Aotearoa New Zealand', in *Pacific Art Niu Sila* (Wellington: Te Papa Press, 2002), 209–25.

Classical Encounters
by Michael Harlow

Athens to Aotearoa: Greece and Rome in New Zealand literature and society, eds Diana Burton, Simon Perris and Jeff Tatum (Victoria University Press, 2018), 360pp, $40

No body of literature or art is innocent of the legacy of its forebears. The Nobel Prizewinning Greek poet Seferis, speaking from Athens about the state of literature and art in his country, said, 'I believe there is no parthenogenesis in art.' He was acknowledging the inescapable influence and impact of classical Greek mythology in shaping the cultural life of his country.

The importance of myth, story and art in forging a national identity is a dynamic one. And reading and writing as complementary activities are an integral part of the 'creation story' that any nation or state wants to tell about itself. Through a miscellany and broad range of voices, including writers, poets, artists, critics and historians, the stated aim of *Athens to Aotearoa: Greece and Rome in New Zealand literature and society* is to 'include investigations of New Zealand's encounter with the classics not only in literature and art but in other aspects of our society as well' (7). The anthology comprises a collection of talks and papers that grew out of the 2014 Victoria University conference in Wellington that shared the title of this anthology. Given the academic provenance of this project, one might expect rather a limited readership. However, the very encouraging news is that the inclusion of papers by and about poets, writers and artists makes this a very good catch for the wider readership that it deserves.

The Introduction by Simon Perris is exemplary—an intelligent and inspired entrée. Perris strikes the resoundingly apt note and conviction that

> beyond doubt classical antiquity still offers an avenue for local writers and other writers to think seriously about identity and selfhood in an increasingly connected global society … More importantly it also speaks to biculturalism and to the need for a more capacious, more nuanced view of what it means to be in and of Aotearoa New Zealand and to live under the sign of Te Tiriti o Waitangi (42).

For readers entering the house of New Zealand's cultural relationship to classical Greece and Rome, at the outset a privileged voice is given to artists and writers: two novelists, two poets and a visual artist. The imaginative voice of literature and art opens with Witi Ihimaera's conference address, whose rhetorical flourishes focus on the 'continuing relevance of classical antiquity for himself, for Māori and indeed for everyone in Aotearoa New Zealand' (36).

Artist Marian Maguire's artwork graces the cover: a lithograph depicting the Greek hero Herakles wrestling with the Māori mythic monster or 'magic being' taniwha. Both classical mythologems translate each other, bridging historical and mythological time. In many ways this is a brilliant, encapsulating narrative 'essay' on its own and can be read as such. The artistic imagination is expressed from the distaff side in her chapter 'A Fabricated History of Graeco-New Zealand Interaction'. As an artist and mythographer Maguire illustrates here not only an historical truth as she sees it, but an artistic and healing truth as well: 'I have come to believe it unhealthy for people, any people, to separate themselves from the myths embedded in their culture. They help us investigate human nature.' It is fascinating to see in her pictorial imagery and in her textual hermeneutic 'encounters between the ancient Greek, Māori and colonial Pākehā milieux' (35). Maguire's artistic vision is further extended in Greta Hawes' 'Discussions with Mountains in Marian Maguire's *A Taranaki Dialogue*': 'The ways in which Socratic wisdom plays out in this series of etchings, and the ways in which a viewer, compelled by Socrates' questions to participate actively in the work, to engage her faculties of reason and imagination … (132)' It is encouraging to have the Great Interrogator Socrates arrive in the Antipodes to join this Symposium.

Simon Perris's muse remains inspirational, with respect to myth, in his keystone essay 'Orpheus, Māui and the Underworld in New Zealand Literature'. Perris discusses the archetypal figure of Orpheus (ur-poet of the classical world) '*vis-à-vis* Māori and Pākehā writers' engagement with Māori and Greek myth' (174). At the centre of this important discussion is the archetypal mythologem the katabasis, the descent to the Underworld. His interpretative reading of the Orpheus-Māui mythos makes for fascinating reading. And it is resonantly consonant with the concept-image of the Nekyia, often portrayed as the *night-sea-journey* in Jungian and post-Jungian symbolic thought. He also calls attention to literary figures such as Ihimaera, James K. Baxter and Robert Sullivan among others, including Anna Seward's *Elegy on Captain Cook* (1780).

A most welcome reference is made to the poet Robert Sullivan's *Captain Cook in the Underworld*—a dramatic poem (originally a libretto) in which the narrative image of the katabasis includes a heroic trio: Cook, Orpheus and Māui. For Sullivan this becomes a mythopoetic way of 'moving from a Greek to a New Zealand archetype' (186). Sullivan's poetic oeuvre is rich with his understanding and his ability to 'translate' classical story and myth to the mythic Māori and Polynesian worldview. His poetic works deserve a closer and deeper interpretative scrutiny. Again, Perris strikes the bell-note: 'Orpheus … is an appropriate model for a New Zealand poet' (187).

As one might expect, the poet, dramatist, short-story writer and self-affirmed pilgrim James K. Baxter is the focus of two critical literary discussions. It is Baxter's proclivity for classical mythology and how it was articulated in his life and work that is on tap here. Geoffrey Miles' take on Baxter's short story 'Venus in Her Western Bed', in which Baxter uses the Venus (Aphrodite)-Anchises story, turns out to be a rather delayed adolescent eros-driven plaint of a failed love affair, 'a funny, sad, embarrassing account of young men behaving badly' (199). Particularly interesting, especially for committed Baxter readers, is Miles' insightful reading, which demonstrates the hermeneutic value of psychological interpretation and critique. There is a psychological intensity in Baxter's work that the poet himself recognised in a letter to poet, priest, editor and spiritual mentor John Weir: 'It seems to me often that each poem is part of a large subconscious *corpus* of personal myth, like an island above the sea …' (215). What is implied here, if not directly stated, is Baxter's fragmented awareness that the Venus-Aphrodite archetype is his *personal myth*. Freud had his Oedipus Complex, Jung his Collective Unconscious, and Baxter his *anima* as core psychic realities.

A clear case might also be made for the Dionysus-Christ imago as root metaphor, both in Baxter's psychic development and his poetic writing.

Attention is also given to Baxter as a playwright in Sharon Matthews' psychologically informed discussion of his play *Dionysus, Christ and the Publican*. According to Baxter the play is based on the death and resurrection of Christ, events that 'have some meaning even for a modern audience' (219).

Here we see Baxter wrestling personally with his often confused and ambiguous projective identification with the Christ archetype. The conflation of the alcoholic-as-godlike-figure of Barry Flanagan with the mythic figure of Dionysus clearly highlights Baxter's use of classical myth and biblical story; and his own psychic struggle, wrestling with the dark angel of his divided self. Matthews calls on the psychoanalyst Hannah Segal's affirmative insight: 'The hidden purpose of creativity is to nurture psychic work' (224).

The scholarly and poetic eye is also focused on Latin/Roman writers. Catullus (with Horace) has had a particularly good profiling in New Zealand for both academics and poets, most notably here in the essay by Maxine Lewis, the scrupulous critical attention of John Davidson's 'Horace, Catullus, Lucretius and Mason', and the chapter by poet Anna Jackson.

Maxine Lewis in her essay 'C.K. Stead Writes Catullus: Persona, Intention, Intratext and Allusion' takes on the sometimes thorny reaction to Stead's use of the persona-voice ('his personal voice'), as a projection of experiences from his personal life. In her discussion of a bad—it's fair to say wayward—review by teacher and reviewer Charles Croot, she also mentions en passant a remark by writer and occasional critic Jack Ross referring to Stead's poetic relationship to Catullus as 'classical ventriloquising' (246, n.10). Many readers will find this discussion (however laboured under the weight of postmodernist, poststructuralist idiom

and theory) particularly interesting because it is in part based on an interview with Stead, giving him ample space to respond to some of the agonistic critical reception of his Catullus poems. Stead is critically astute in clearing away some of the 'dead wood' surrounding much of this negative criticism. He is clear about his use of the Catullus persona and his own interpretative voice; and his reply to his *agonistes* is intelligently persuasive. The essay also raises the perennial issue of what translation is and does as poetic practice. As a community of readers, we need to have more informed and first-hand critical commentary about this. And there is also some talk about the complex and fugitive notion of *authorial intention*.

John Davidson's critical appraisal of poet R.A.K. Mason, of 'almost legendary status as New Zealand's first distinctively original poet writing in English', is at the centre of his essay. Davidson identifies for the reader a central preoccupation of Mason's poetry, 'the sombre cadences of mortality' (referring to A.E. Housman's *A Shropshire Lad*). 'This feature is central for Mason's work too' (269). Davidson's essay is intellectually discerning, scrupulous in its scholarship and close reading; and with admirable clarity in a language free of the coded jargon of poststructuralist theory so freighted with elitist presumptions. Clarity of thought presented with a clarity of language.

To those interested or just curious about the historical and early classical connection to Aotearoa New Zealand's thought and literature, Peter Whiteford takes a close textual look at Anna Seward's *Elegy on Captain Cook* (1780). 'This is to the best of my knowledge, the first literary work in English explicitly to name New Zealand ... Seward thus has the distinction of being the first person to link Athens to Aotearoa, from the somewhat unusual position of never having seen either' (297). Whiteford's knowledge is extensive and his clear thinking makes this an amiable, admirable and readable essay.

Under the sectional rubric *History and Society*, Matthew Trundle weighs in with 'a brief survey [in which] I want to show how classical literature, mythology and history played a role in framing the military context of New Zealanders at war' (313). I found it particularly interesting how Trundle points to the imperialistic idealisation of militant heroism as a continuing influence on the collective expression of New Zealand identity—the archetypal hero again, inescapably so in whatever guise.

The anthology concludes, rather fittingly, with an 'overview of the current state of Classics education in New Zealand' by Arlene Holmes-Henderson (326). In her thorough, comparative research study, Holmes-Henderson registers the current and relative popularity of classical studies, now 'a mainstream subject', and lamentably the continuing decline of Latin and the 'almost non-existent teaching of Classical Greek' (327). This is a welcome and clearly informative clarion call (however muted) to think about and do something about the moribund state of affairs when it comes to the teaching of classical subjects: 'It is hoped that all those committed to preserving and expanding access to classical subjects in schools will support each other by sharing examples of "what works" and "what does not work"' (344).

Athens to Aotearoa, Alpha-to-Alpha, may well be a good—even ground-breaking—opportunity for writers and readers, artists and students and teachers, and anyone else who cares about or is just curious about the thought and culture of those-who-have-come-before, and how it contributes to who we imagine we are coming to be. Time, then, to join or rejoin the symposium.

Resonant and Relevant

by Emma Gattey, Awhina Clark-Tahana and Jacinta Ruru

Juridical Encounters: Māori and the colonial courts 1840–1852 by Shaunnagh Dorsett (Auckland University Press, 2017), 320pp, $49.99

This is a book about law and our first courts. It is a book about the interface between two legal systems: Māori and British. And it is a book about the power struggle for colonial legal dominance. This book goes to the heart of issues of nation-making and provides us all with a fascinating context against which to better understand how 'the concerns of the past are still the concerns of the present and how legal frameworks and legal techniques are enduring'. It asks big questions and makes us confront the fallacious notion that Māori law has no force and no validity then or now. Dorsett concludes: 'It is, rather, a question of whether we care to hear it [tikanga Māori] speak.' What a delightful conclusion and one that, along with the whole tenor and freshness of this book, we applaud.

To get to this conclusion, Dorsett begins her book with the telling of the first sitting of the newly established New Zealand Supreme Court in early 1842. It is a sad and horrific case of murder. A Ngā Puhi man, Maketū Wharetōtara (also known as Wiremu Kīngi Maketū), was convicted and sentenced to death for the murder of his employer and her family. It is an interesting case because Maketū's family gave him up to be tried under the British law. Is this a classic example of Māori willingly surrendering their own law? *Juridical Encounters* seeks to understand more deeply whether this is so.

Dorsett forecasts early on that '[t]he rhetoric and the reality were somewhat different'. She accepts that Māori lived under and according to their own laws, and while the British asserted sovereignty over the country in 1840, it hardly meant in the eyes of Māori that British law was automatically legitimate or even effective in Māori communities. Prior to 1840, the Europeans had recognised Māori sovereignty and Māori laws. Post-1840, Māori still expected to know and practise their laws, but the arriving British began transforming the country to render it 'fit for settler colonisation'. The British felt they had to import their law *and* impress it on Māori. Where and how this first happened is well told here.

Juridical Encounters shines a new spotlight on the day-to-day civil and criminal actions in our embryonic courts. Far from being mundane, these regular matters—drunkenness, debt recovery, larceny, assault—are significant sites of encounter in the new colony. The courts back then were places of social engagement, of 'noise and disorder'. Citizens, including Māori, often came into court out of curiosity. Cases were enthusiastically reported in local newspapers. But also, as places of law, the colonial courts were a crucial site of assimilatory practice, underpinned by 'exceptionalism': the doctrine of exempting Indigenous peoples from the full application of a new legal system.

Spanning from the signing of Te Tiriti o Waitangi in 1840 to 1852, this work shows how Māori were first subjected to British law and how the New Zealand legal system was transformed through exceptional, modified laws.

Juridical Encounters is broken into three parts. Part I, entitled 'Whose Law? Which Law?', considers the ideological challenges the colonial officials faced in integrating British law into New Zealand. Law was seen as an 'agent of change', a prime mover of assimilation and protection to placate, protect and 'civilise' Indigenous peoples. Decisions had to be made about what kinds of matters the settler courts should have jurisdiction over, what these courts might look like, and how Māori could be brought before them.

The 'bricks and mortar' segment, Part II, entitled 'Designing Exceptional Laws and Institutions', assesses the motivations and successes of the exceptional regimes proposed by Lieutenant-Governor Hobson, Governors Fitzroy and Grey, and the Chief Protector of Aborigines, George Clarke. By exploring the spectrum of opinions of 'Māori amenability to British law and institutional design' and the diverse range of ideas for designing legal institutions in the new colony (including those which were not implemented), Dorsett reveals the contingency of the resultant legal system and its features.

Part III examines 'exceptionalism in action' by analysing these regimes, the supporting institutions and the micro-level interactions in the practice of the criminal courts and the Resident Magistrates' Courts. Dorsett identifies the Protector of Aborigines and his allied officers (lawyers and interpreters) as a significant means of tracking Māori participation in the court system, as these individuals were a crucial interface between Māori and British law and the settler courts. Her conclusion, illustrated through numerous case studies, is that Māori were proactive presences in court but that ultimately 'the coming of Māori to these new institutions had the effect of beginning the slow displacement of traditional adjudicatory fora, and consequently, the places from which Māori law could speak'.

Scrutinising parliamentary and public debates of the period, Dorsett challenges the view of colonisation as a fatalistic and inevitable wave that systematically swept New Zealand into the British system. Particular attention is paid to *inter se* matters (those between Māori, rather than those involving settlers) and the surrounding confusion as to whether these matters would, or should, be subject to British law. Essentially, Dorsett advances a theory of jurisdictional pointillism, whereby customary law was gradually displaced by the accretion of petty proceedings. This deliberate incrementalism was firmly grounded in socio-economic, political and legal theory, and tied to goals of assimilation and 'civilisation'.

In a 'brief jurisprudential afterword', Dorsett weaves together the statistics and factual patterns exposed and explored throughout the book to show that the displacement of tikanga was not a seismic moment but a slow, complex and non-linear process, cemented over time through the many micro-encounters between Māori and the lower courts. Dorsett then shifts time periods to today, to two contemporary Supreme Court decisions where the question of whether Māori law should have any influence in the courts' decision-making as modern examples of 'problematizing the meeting of peoples and laws'. This epilogue traces the accretion of common law jurisdiction, its arrogation of tūrangawaewae, and the proportional ousting of tikanga Māori, which Dorsett emphasises has been displaced, not extinguished. She challenges us to ask not whether tikanga Māori retains any force or validity, but whether we—and our historically contingent, value-laden institutions—care to hear it speak. As Māori continue to interact kanohi ki te kanohi (face to face) with courts modelled on theories of assimilation and civilisation, this is a resonant message for our times, marking *Juridical Encounters* as an outstanding and relevant book for wide readership.

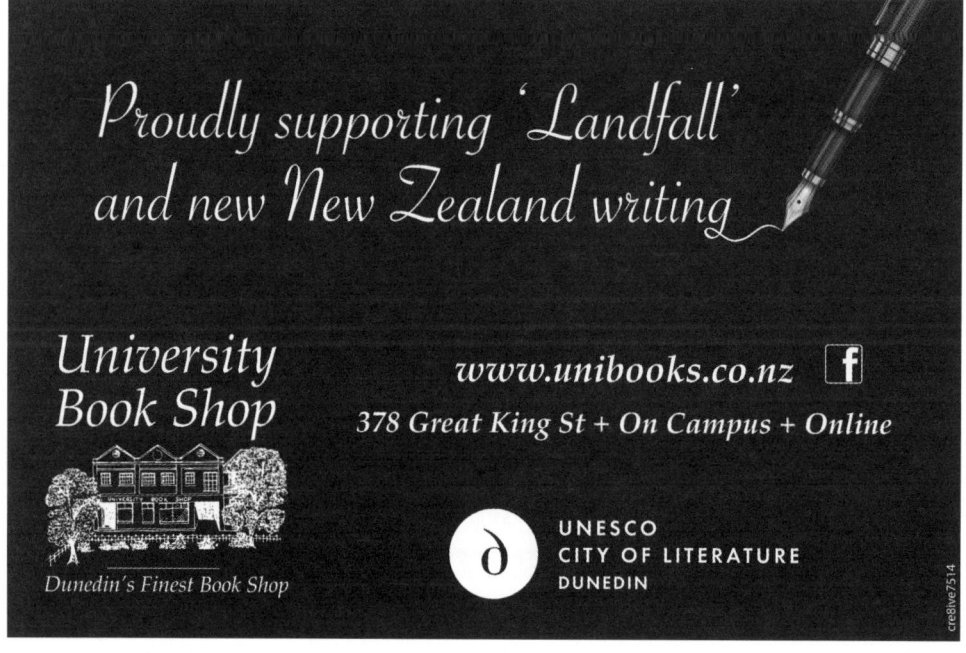

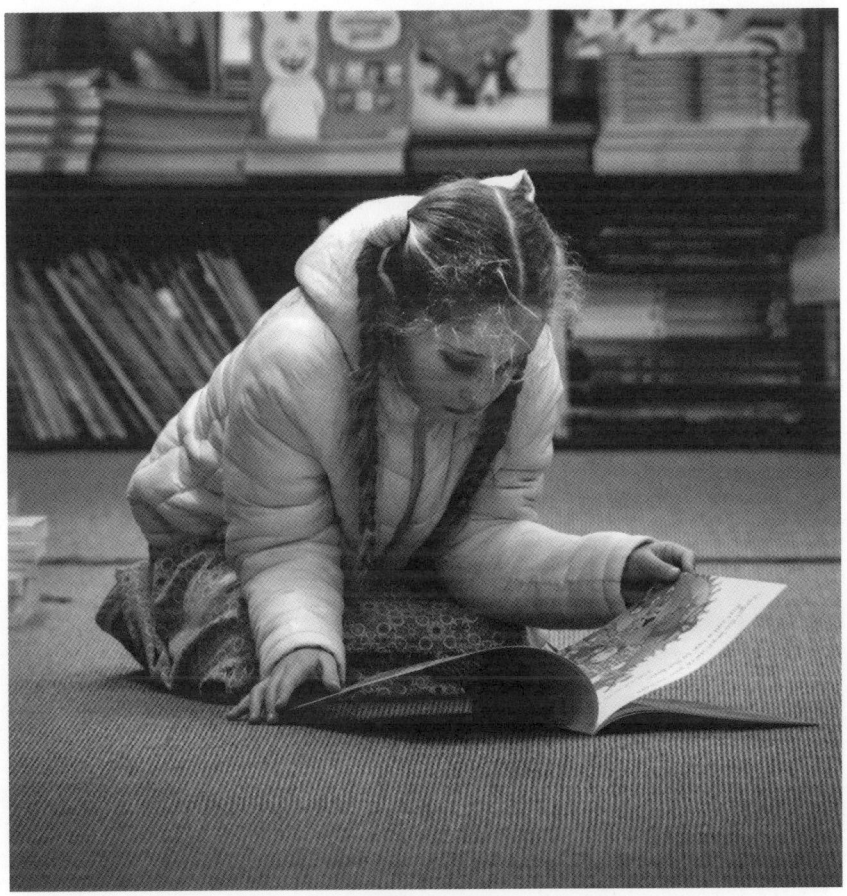

future Landfall editor swots up

UNITY BOOKS

57 Willis Street, Wellington | 19 High St, Auckland
04 499 4245 | 09 307 0731
wellington@unitybooks.co.nz | auckland@unitybooks.co.nz
www.unitybooksonline.co.nz

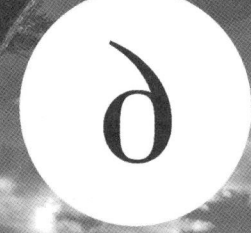

new from Victoria University Press

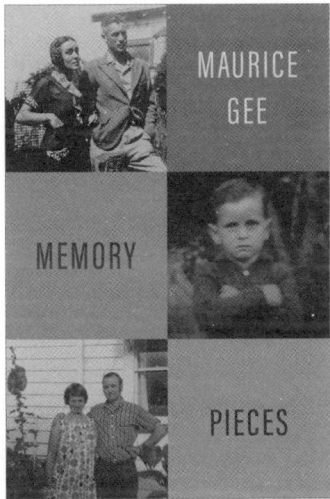

An intimate and evocative memoir by New Zealand's leading living writer.
Memoir, pb, $35

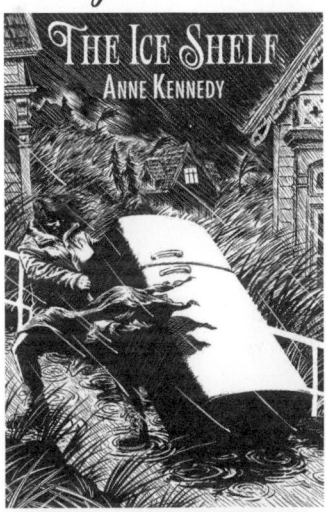

An electrifying allegory for the dangers of wasting love and other non-renewable resources. Novel, pb, $30

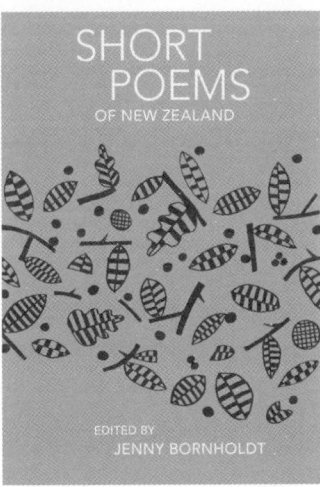

A short poem can contain the world. This anthology celebrates the power and many moods of the form.
Poetry, hb, $35

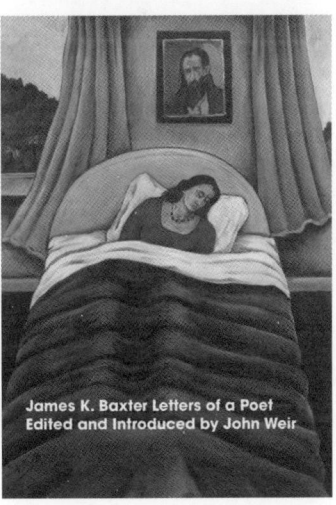

Frank, funny, generous, sometimes filthy, Baxter's letters give insight into his life and work.
Letters, hb, 2 vol. boxed set, $100

NEW BOOKS FROM
OTAGO

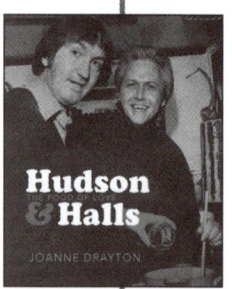

HUDSON & HALLS: THE FOOD OF LOVE
JOANNE DRAYTON

Hudson and Halls were pioneers of celebrity television who rocketed to stardom on untrained talent and a dream. In this fast-paced and meticulously researched book, New York Times-bestselling author Joanne Drayton celebrates the legacy of this unforgettable duo.
ISBN 978-1-98-853126-7, paperback, $49.95

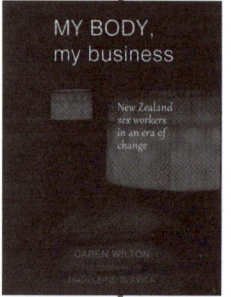

MY BODY, MY BUSINESS: NZ SEX WORKERS IN AN ERA OF CHANGE
CAREN WILTON with photographs by MADELEINE SLAVICK

Eleven former and current New Zealand sex workers speak frankly, in their own voices, about their lives in and out of the sex industry. Their stories are by turns eye-opening, poignant, heartening, disturbing and compelling.
ISBN 978-1-98-853132-8, paperback, $45

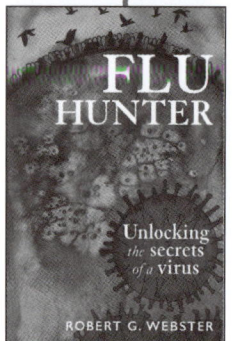

FLU HUNTER: UNLOCKING THE SECRETS OF A VIRUS
ROBERT G. WEBSTER

When a new influenza virus emerges that is able to be transmitted between humans, it spreads globally as a pandemic, often with high mortality. The 1918 Spanish influenza pandemic was undoubtedly the most devastating influenza pandemic to date, and it has been Dr Robert Webster's life's work to figure out how and why, before the next one strikes.
ISBN 978-1-98-853131-1, paperback, $35

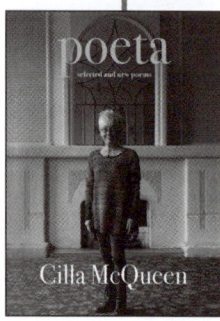

POETA: SELECTED AND NEW POEMS
CILLA McQUEEN

Bringing together a definitive selection of the work of a leading New Zealand poet spanning five decades, arranged by the author in a thematic narrative that elucidates abiding themes while maintaining a loose chronology of her creative life to date.
ISBN 978-1-98-853128-1, hardback, $39.95

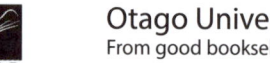

Otago University Press
From good booksellers or www.otago.ac.nz/press

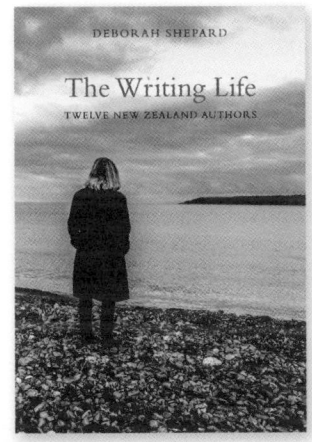

Joy Cowley • Marilyn Duckworth
Tessa Duder • Chris Else • Patricia Grace
David Hill • Witi Ihimaera • Fiona Kidman
Owen Marshall • Vincent O'Sullivan
Philip Temple • Albert Wendt

Twelve of New Zealand's most acclaimed and admired writers speak candidly about their lives and their work.

Out in November 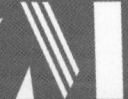 MASSEY UNIVERSITY PRESS

LAUREATE'S CHOICE chosen by CAROL ANN DUFFY

Pamper Me to Hell & Back

HERA LINDSAY BIRD

"New Zealand's most exciting new poet"
– the Guardian

available from www.poetrybusiness.co.uk

CONTRIBUTORS

Philip Armstrong teaches at Canterbury University. His poetry and short fiction have appeared in Landfall, Sport, Snorkel, PN Review and elsewhere. His most recent book is Sheep (Reaktion, 2016).

Jane Arthur is a Wellington-based poet and editor. She has an MA in creative writing from the IIML at Victoria University and won the 2018 Sarah Broom Poetry Prize.

Tusiata Avia is a poet, writer and performer. She has published three collections of poetry, a chapbook and three children's books. She wrote and performed a one-woman show, Wild Dogs Under My Skirt, which she toured 2002–08, and in 2016 it became an award-winning play for six women. Tusiata has held a number of awards and writers' residencies and has performed at literary festivals around the globe. Her latest book, Fale Aitu | Spirit House, was a finalist for the Ockham NZ Book Awards in 2017.

Antonia Bale is a short-story writer from Wellington, a city that finds its way into many of her stories. She has an MA with distinction in creative writing from the IIML at Victoria University.

Tony Beyer operates out of Taranaki. Anchor Stone (Cold Hub Press, 2017) was a finalist in the poetry category of the 2018 Ockham NZ Book Awards. New work has appeared this year in broadsheet, Landfall, Otoliths and Poetry Pacific.

Victor Billot lives in Dunedin. He has published three poetry collections, including Ambient Terror (2017). His work has recently been published in Cordite, Meniscus, Minarets, The Spinoff and takahē.

Formerly books and culture editor for the NZ Listener, **Mark Broatch** is a journalist, author and stay-at-home dad.

Tom Brooking is a professor of history at the University of Otago and is currently working on an edited set of essays on culture and democracy, as well as a book on the making of rural New Zealand.

Janet Charman's Smoking: The homoerotic subtext of Man Alone, a matrixial reading is available as a free download from www.genrebooks.co.nz. Her latest collection of poems is ꤅ Surrender (OUP, 2017).

Madeleine Child lives in Dunedin, hoping it will warm up. She has a couple of sons and a dog. She is surprised to find writing not so very different from working with clay.

Awhina Clark-Tahana (Te Arawa) is a law and history student and part-time research assistant at the University of Otago. She has held a legal research internship at Otago where she focused on Māori legal experiences of the Wildlife Act 1953.

Gina Cole, of Fijian, Scottish and Welsh descent, lives in Tāmaki Makarau, Aotearoa. In 2013 she completed an MCW at Auckland University. Her writing has been published in various literary magazines and anthologies. Her debut book of short stories, Black Ice Matter (Huia, 2016), won the Hubert Church Prize for Best First Book at the 2017 Ockham NZ Book Awards. She is a PhD candidate at Massey University, researching speculative fiction and science fiction in Oceania.

Thom Conroy is the author of two novels, The Salted Air and The Naturalist (both Penguin Random House), and is the editor of the essay collection Home (Massey University Press). His short fiction, widely

CONTRIBUTORS

published in New Zealand and the US, has been recognised by *Best American Short Stories 2012* and has received other awards, including the Katherine Ann Porter Prize in Fiction and the Sunday Star-Times Short Fiction Competition. He is a senior lecturer in creative writing at Massey University.

Jodie Dalgleish is a writer, curator and sonic artist living in Luxembourg. She is returning to her own practice after more than a decade curating within New Zealand's art museum sector. She has been published online and in print in numerous arts-related publications.

Doc Drumheller was born in Charleston, South Carolina, and has lived in New Zealand for more than half his life. He has worked in award-winning groups for theatre and music and has published 10 collections of poetry. His poems have been translated into more than 20 languages. He lives in Oxford, where he edits and publishes the literary journal *Catalyst*.

Breton Dukes lives in Dunedin with his wife and two boys. He has published two collections of stories with VUP. He hopes to publish a new collection next year.

David Eggleton received the Janet Frame Literary Trust Award for Poetry in 2015. His collection of poems, *The Conch Trumpet*, won the 2016 Ockham NZ Book Award for Poetry. His latest collection, *Edgeland and other poems*, was published by Otago University Press in July 2018. Formerly editor of *Landfall*, David is currently Pasifika Writer in Residence at the University of Hawai`i at Mānoa.

Ciaran Fox has been helping organise the literary arts journal *Catalyst* since 2003. He is host of their infamous long-running poetry open mics in Christchurch and many other events, and has appeared in various literary and music festivals and occasionally with the Lyttelton Poets.

Emma Gattey is a junior barrister in Wellington. She studied law and history at the University of Otago, delving deeply into the intersection of tikanga Māori and the common law. She recently published work in *Eugenics at the Edges of Empire* (Palgrave Macmillan, 2018) and *Feminist Judgments of Aotearoa* (Bloomsbury, 2017).

David Gregory has had three books published, *Always Arriving* and *Frame of Mind* (Sudden Valley Press) and *Push* (Black Doris Press). His poetry has appeared in many publications and anthologies, and he has performed his work here and in the UK.

Michael Hall lives in Dunedin. Recent poems of his have appeared in *takahē*, *Queens Quarterly* and *The Spinoff*.

Michael Harlow is a writer, editor, librettist and Jungian therapist living in Central Otago. He is a longtime student of Classical Greek language and literature and has just received the Prime Minister's Award for Literary Achievement in Poetry.

René Harrison's poetry and essays have appeared in *Literary Orphans*, *Landfall*, *takahē*, *Poetry New Zealand*, *Wordgathering*, *Shot Glass Journal*, *Blackmail Press* and *Brief*, among other places. He has taught literature and rhetoric at Auckland University and Purdue University.

Siobhan Harvey is the author of five books, including the poetry collection *Cloudboy* (Otago University Press, 2014), which won the Kathleen Grattan Award. She's also co-editor of *Essential New Zealand Poems* (Penguin Random House, 2014). Recently, her poetry, fiction and creative nonfiction have been published in *Arc* (Canada), *Asian Literary Review* (Hong Kong), *Griffith Review*

(Aus), *Segue* (US), *Stand* (UK), *Structo* (UK), *takahē* and in *Manifesto Aotearoa: 101 political poems* (Otago University Press, 2016). She won the 2016 Write Well Award (Fiction, US) and was runner-up in the 2015 and 2014 New Zealand Poetry Society International Poetry Competitions.

Trevor Hayes lives in Punakaiki. His debut chapbook, *Two Lagoons*, was published by Seraph Press in 2017.

Kerry Hines is a Wellington-based poet, writer and researcher. Her poetry collection *Young Country* (with photographs by William Williams) was published by Auckland University Press in 2014.

Joy Holley is from Wellington and is currently studying at Victoria University. Her writing has also appeared in *Starling*, *Headland* and The Spinoff.

Elizabeth Kirkby-McLeod has an MA in creative writing with first-class honours and has had poetry published in New Zealand. She has a children's book forthcoming with a New Zealand publisher.

Megan Kitching lives in Dunedin and tutors English and creative writing at the University of Otago. Her poetry has appeared in *The Frogmore Papers* (UK), *Critic* and the *Otago Daily Times*.

Jessica Le Bas has published two collections of poetry, *incognito* and *Walking to Africa* (Auckland University Press, 2007, 2009), and a novel for children (*Staying Home*, Penguin, 2010). She currently lives and works in the Cook Islands.

Therese Lloyd is the author of two full-length collections of poetry, *Other Animals* and *The Facts* (Victoria University Press, 2013, 2018). She has a doctorate in creative writing from Victoria University and is the 2018 University of Waikato Writer in Residence.

Jess MacKenzie has a love for words, character, and the boundaries of genre. She writes stories of varying length and form, as well as the odds and ends that come through to freelance copywriters. Her short stories have appeared in a number of journals.

Frankie McMillan is a short-story writer and poet. Her recent book *My Mother and the Hungarians and other small fictions* was long-listed in the 2017 Ockham NZ Book Awards.

Alice Miller's new collection of poems, *Nowhere Nearer*, was co-published by Auckland University Press and Liverpool University Press (2018). She lives in Berlin.

Michael Mintrom is a New Zealander living in Melbourne. Best known for his academic writing, he has published poetry in Australian and New Zealand journals including *Landfall*, *Quadrant* and *Sport*. He is a past winner of the University of Canterbury's Macmillan Brown Prize for Writers.

Lissa Moore emigrated from the UK in 2003 with her husband and three children, and currently works part time as a learning support tutor in Dunedin. Her poems have appeared in *Tiny Gaps* (NZ) and *Reactions* (UK).

James Norcliffe has published nine collections of poetry including *Shadow Play* (2013) and *Dark Days at the Oxygen Café* (2016). Recent work has appeared in *Acumen*, *The Cincinnati Review*, *Salamander*, *Gargoyle* and *Flash Fiction International* (Norton, 2015). With Michelle Elvy and Frankie McMillan he recently edited *Bonsai: Best small stories from Aotearoa New Zealand*

(Canterbury University Press, 2018). He is currently the writer in residence at the Randell Cottage, Wellington, and has a new collection forthcoming with Otago University Press.

Heidi North's poetry and short stories have been published in NZ, Australia, the US and the UK. She won an international Irish award for her poetry in 2007, and has won New Zealand awards for her short fiction. Her first poetry book, *Possibility of Flight*, was published by Mākaro Press in 2015. Heidi joined the Shanghai International Writers Program as the NZ fellow in September–October in 2016. She was awarded the Hachette/NZSA mentorship in 2017 to work on her first novel.

Jilly O'Brien is a Dunedin poet and psychologist. She has had poems published in The Spinoff, *Otago Daily Times*, Blackmail Press, and anthologies such as *Bread & Roses* (UK) and *Penguin Days* and *Ice Diver* (NZPS). She is part of the Dunedin heritage collaboration of artists, and one of her poems is etched into a bench in the warehouse precinct there. She recently won the Robert Burns poetry competition 2017/18.

Vincent O'Sullivan's recent work includes the novel *All This by Chance*, the poetry collection *And So It Is* and the oratorio *Face* with composer Ross Harris, performed by the Auckland Philharmonic Orchestra and Voices New Zealand, and the BBC Symphony and Choir, earlier this year. He lives in Dunedin.

Gail Pittaway is a senior lecturer at Wintec, Hamilton. She has published poetry and short stories as well as articles, chapters and papers on creative writing, New Zealand literature, the history of food writing, New Zealand cookery books and crime writing. She is a regular theatre critic for Theatreview website.

Aiwa Pooamorn is a Thai-Chinese mother, poet and theatre performer. She has featured in Poetry Live and performed her poems as part of Alice Canton's award-winning theatre show *Other [Chinese]*.

Born in Napier, **John Prins** is a writer living in Auckland. He is currently writing a novel in the space between new fatherhood and sleep.

Lindsay Rabbitt was born in Invercargill and raised in Alexandra but is mostly domiciled in the Wellington region, presently on the Kapiti Coast.

essa may ranapiri (takatāpui; they/them/theirs) is a poet from Kirikiriroa, Aotearoa. They have words in *Mayhem*, *Poetry NZ*, *Brief*, *Starling*, *THEM* and *POETRY Magazine*. They will write until they're dead.

Sudha Rao completed her MA in creative writing at Victoria University of Wellington in 2017. Originally from South India, Sudha has a dance background and spent her early New Zealand years in Dunedin. She is a University of Otago graduate and now lives in Wellington.

Richard Reeve lives in Warrington. His last book of poems was *Generation Kitchen* (OUP, 2015).

Harry Ricketts teaches English literature and creative non-fiction at Victoria University of Wellington. He has published around thirty books, including eleven collections of poetry (most recently *Winter Eyes*, VUP, 2018).

John Z Robinson is a Foxton-born jeweller and artist. He has lived in Dunedin and Kaitangata since the late 1970s.

Alan Roddick is a Dunedin poet whose latest book, *Getting It Right*, was published by Otago University Press in 2016. As Charles Brasch's literary executor, he has also edited three collections of Brasch's poems.

Jacinta Ruru (Raukawa, Ngāti Ranginui) lives in Dunedin where she teaches law at the University of Otago. She is co-director of Ngā Pae o te Māramatanga, New Zealand's Māori Centre of Research Excellence, a fellow of the Royal Society Te Apārangi, and a recipient of the Prime Minister's Supreme Award for Excellence in Tertiary Teaching.

Derek Schulz is a poet, essayist and writer of fictions. His poem 'you can't be here' pays homage to friend and workmate Jean Webster. Arohanui Gem!

Justin Spiers is a Dunedin-based artist working predominantly with photography. In 2017 he won the Cleveland National Art Award and was a finalist in both the Wallace Art Awards and the National Contemporary Art Awards. In 2018 he was the Caselberg Trust Creative Connections resident where he continued the Pet Photo Booth project. Justin was director of the Perth Centre for Photography from 2004–07 and has exhibited in galleries throughout Australasia, including the Australian Centre for Photography, Perth Institute of Contemporary Art, the Art Gallery of Western Australia, A Gallery, National Portrait Gallery, State of Princes and Dunedin Public Art Gallery.

Di Starrenburg has an MA in creative writing from the University of Auckland. She won the Sir James Wallace Prize for her thesis and her stories have since appeared in literary journals in NZ and the US.

Jillian Sullivan lives in Central Otago. She has published in a wide variety of genres and teaches writing in NZ and the US. Her awards include the 2017 NZSA Beatson Fellowship and the Highlights Fiction Award (US).

John Summers is the author of the non-fiction collection *The Mermaid Boy* (Hue & Cry, 2015). His writing has previously appeared in *Landfall* as well as *Sport*, *North & South*, *New Zealand Listener* and *The Spinoff*.

Jasmine O.M. Taylor from Dunedin has won and been placed in a number of local poetry competitions, and happily shares her work at open mic evenings hosted by the Octagon Poetry Collective each month.

Susan Te Kahurangi King was born in Te Aroha in 1951. Primarily known for her drawings on paper, she is also active in painting and needlework. A prolific drawer for most of her life, Susan showed signs of talent at a very early age but in the early 1990s ceased drawing completely. In 2008, however, fuelled by interest in her work, she once again began to draw, continuing where she had left off. Since this reawakening she has become prolific. Earlier this year the Museum of Modern Art, New York, confirmed the acquisition of three of her drawings, making Susan only the second New Zealand artist to have their work directly acquired by the institution.

Angela Trolove works seasonally harvesting fruit, and as a waitress. In her writing she searches for absolute honesty, often tailoring her present-day experiences into old verse forms. Her poems have been published in *Blackmail Press*, and in *Best New Zealand Poems* (Victoria University Press).

Iain Twiddy grew up in eastern England, studied literature at university, and lived for several years in northern Japan. His poetry has been accepted by a number of publications, including *The London Magazine* and *The Honest Ulsterman*.

Bryan Walpert is author of three collections of poetry, most recently *Native Bird* (Mākaro Press, 2015). He is an associate professor of creative writing at Massey University in Auckland.

Susan Wardell is from Dunedin. She has a doctorate in social anthropology and communication studies from the University of Otago, where she now lectures. She is raising two small human beings and a few potted plants. Her poetry has been published in *Landfall*, *takahē* and *The Scribbler*.

Rose Whitau is Kāi Tahu, Kāti Mamoe, Waitaha and Pākehā, and has been living in various parts of Australia for the past six years.

C.A.J. Williams was born in the port village of Bluff. He took degrees from Massey University and the University of Otago. His first poetry collection, *35 Short Poems*, appeared in 2016. His second collection, *50 Historical Footnotes*, is due in 2019. He lives in Wellington.

Briar Wood grew up in South Auckland and worked in Britain until 2012. She currently lives in Northland, where she draws inspiration for her writing from many sources.

Helen Yong's work has been published in journals and anthologies, including *After the Cyclone* (NZPS, 2017), *Leaving the Red Zone* (Clerestory Press, 2016), *JAAM*, *takahē*, *Kokako* and *Eucalypt* (Australia).

CONTRIBUTIONS

Landfall publishes original poems, essays, short stories, excerpts from works of fiction and non-fiction in progress, reviews, articles on the arts, and portfolios by artists. Written submissions must be typed. Email to landfall@otago.ac.nz with 'Landfall submission' in the subject line, or post to the address below.

Visit our website www.otago.ac.nz/press/landfall/index.html for further information.

SUBSCRIPTIONS

Landfall is published in May and November. The subscription rates for 2018 (two issues) are: New Zealand $55 (including GST); Australia $NZ65; rest of the world $NZ70. Sustaining subscriptions help to support New Zealand's longest running journal of arts and letters, and the writers and artists it showcases. These are in two categories: Friend: between $NZ75 and $NZ125 per year. Patron: $NZ250 and above.

Send subscriptions to Otago University Press, PO Box 56, Dunedin, New Zealand. For enquiries, email landfall@otago.ac.nz or call 64 3 479 8807.

Print ISBN: 978-1-98-853155-7
ePDF ISBN: 978-1-98-853156-4
ISSN 00-23-7930

Copyright © Otago University Press 2018

Published by Otago University Press, Level 1, 398 Cumberland Street, Dunedin, New Zealand.

Typeset by Otago University Press. Printed in New Zealand by Caxton.

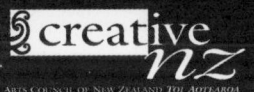

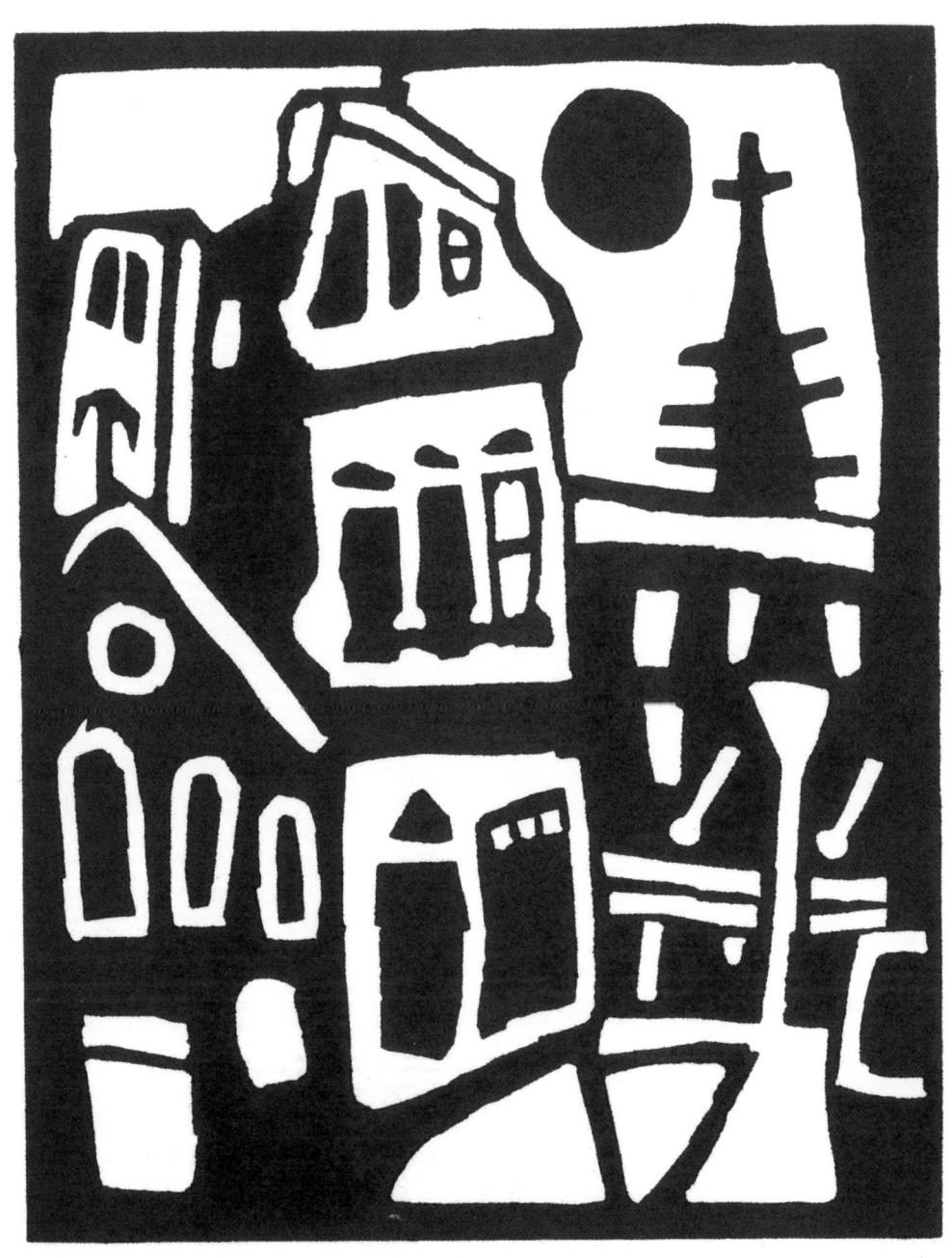

John Z Robinson, *First Church with Scaffolding from Bath Street*. Linocut, 180 x 140 mm, 2018.